To
May The Roads You
Travel be Smooth
Regards
Colin Hansen

Life, Love And Heartache...
Poems of the Northern Lights

Calvin Harasemchuk

AuthorHouse™
1663 Liberty Drive, Suite 200
Bloomington, IN 47403
www.authorhouse.com
Phone: 1-800-839-8640

© *2008 Calvin Harasemchuk. All rights reserved.*

No part of this book may be reproduced, stored in a retrieval system, or transmitted by any means without the written permission of the author.

First published by AuthorHouse 6/23/2008

ISBN: 978-1-4343-9386-9 (sc)
ISBN: 978-1-4343-9387-6 (hc)

Library of Congress Control Number: 2008905582

Printed in the United States of America
Bloomington, Indiana

This book is printed on acid-free paper.

Acknowledgements:

I wish to express my thanks and gratitude to the following people in my life.
Mrs. Clara Lund, May you rest in peace, you encouraged me, as your student. For that I am eternally grateful.
My Love of my life Frances, Your Love means so much to me!
My First Love, Who shall remain unnamed, Thank You!
The other Loves lost, Thank You!
Teresa, My friend, Thank You! We've been through the hard times together.
Ed You married a Great Girl!
The rest of my family, Chris and his wife Jenn, Will, Thank You!
My In-laws, Bill and Bonnie King, Thanks for making me part of your life!
Gordon Quinton, A Big Thank You! You've always been there for me, As I'm always there for you.
And one person, who wants to remain anonymous, Thanks!
Darren Moore, Of Harlequin, not the books! The Band, Thanks!
Jodi Von, Thanks! For your honesty. And the rest of my Facebook friends.
So many others, from my childhood days in Laclu, Thank You!
And…. Jane Knutsen, Thank You! Your encouragement was appreciated.
And See, Dreams Do Become Reality! Wow! What a Ride!

Calvin Harasemchuk   2008

Chapter One- First Love

The First Kiss

As We Walk,
We Talk,
Words Come So Freely,
Words That Have Meaning,
Wind Blowing Our Hair,
She's So Fair,
Holding Hands,
Walking In The Sand,
Little Giggles,
I Hang On To Every Word,
Eyes So Alluring,
Wind Blows Hard, Sand In Her Eye, So Hurts,
I Brush Her Eye, So Carefully,
Tears Come, So Gently,
Arms Come Around My Neck,
I Was Taken Aback,
Did Not Pull Away,
Oh! Lips Brushed Lips, So Soft They Came This Way,
The First Kiss,
Oh! The Bliss....
It Makes Me Feel Warm To This Day...

As Time Goes By

As Time Goes By,
I Think Of You And I,
Many A Word Unspoken,
Of Love That Can Not Be Denied,
Many Words, Better Left Unsaid,
Of The Love That Is Dead,
Honestly I Hoped It Would Never End,
If That Is What You Want,
I Will Always Will Still Love You!
Tears I Have Cried,
Many Times,
Like A River, They Flow,
Down My Cheeks They Go,
As Time Goes By,
I Think Of You And I,
Why Did It End This Way?
I Wish You Would Have Stayed,
Because True Love Never Ends,
It Will Depend,
On What You Feel,
This Broken Dream,
Will Never Finish For Me,
I Will Love You, Forever In My Dreams…….

Lost Love

Just A Day,
So Long Ago,
Was A Warm Summer's Day,
So, Oh So Long Ago,
Not A Day Goes By,
I Think Of You,
First Love, So True,
You Told Me, We are Through,
It Seemed Unreal, I Thought Not True!
Total Innocence, For I Thought, It Was Forever,
I Cried….. Never!
Just A Day,
So Long Ago,
It Was To Be Forever,
Those Words Of Hate Ripped My Heart,
I Couldn't Be Apart,
Walking Did I, Into The Forest So Green,
Thoughts Of Ending, It Seemed,
Words of Hurt,
Wrecking My Heart,
My Gun In My Hand,
Hopefully People Will Understand,
This Broken Heart, The Ache,
Throw This Life Away,
It Just Seemed Right This Way,
Just A Day,
So Long Ago,
Lost Love

So Better This Way,

So It Goes,
I Thought Love Was To Be,
This First Love For Me
Just A Day So Long Ago,
Was A Warm Summer's Day,
As I Sat And Thought,
I Soon Became Overwrought,
The Pain, So Real,
The Real Deal, Forever Love,
As The Sun's Warmth Came,
Thoughts I Overcame,
Live In Pain, Life Goes On,
The Pain Soon Faded, It Was Gone,
So Long Ago, A Piece Of My Heart,
Forever It Remains,
The Pain, Not The Same,
A Long Time Before Love Again,
Burnt Bad, Trust Questions, Never To Surrender,
Of That Day, So Long Ago.
For I Thought, Love Was To Be Forever True,
First Love, To Be True,
Now A Faded Memory,
My Personal Victory

Many A Tear

Many A Tear,
Has Been Cried Over You, My Dear,
Over This Love Of Ours,
Many An Hour,
Spent Contemplating,
Many A Time Hesitating,
What About, The Next Move,
To Take, Over You,
If This Love Be True,
I Know In My Heart,
Never To Be Apart,
Many A Tear,
Has Been Cried Over You, My Dear,
So Far Yet, So Near,
That Day Soon To Appear,
I Give You My Word,
Oh! Be Still, My Heart!
I Will Come To You,
For I Will Always, Love You…

Rain Comes

The Rain Comes,
It Soon Washes Away The Tears,
You Have Gone,
I Wish The Best For You, My Dear,
This Wrecked Heart, I Hold Next To Me,
I Can't Deny,
I'm So Crying,
For My Love Is Simple And Pure,
My Love For You,
The Rain Comes,
Little Tears Become Rivers Flowing,
Rain Drops Falling, Over My Heart, So Falling,
Thoughts Of A Love Gone Wrong,
Words Playing In My Head, Like A Song,
My Hearts So Burning,
I Have Such A Yearning,
The Rain Comes,
Can It Be Undone?
This Love Gone Wrong,
Night Becomes Day,
And I Still Feel This Way,
I Will Remember, The Rain,
And The Pain..

A Broken Heart

A Broken Heart, It May Be,
The Choice It Seems,
Choose Reality,
Or Choose Fantasy,
Two Choices, One To Be Made,
Which Choice Do We Make?
Complacent Or Passion?
Which Gives Satisfaction?
A Broken Heart, It May Be,
For It To Be,
We Have To Be Free,
Close Friends, We Remain,
Regardless Of This Broken Dream,
If We Choose Reality!
In Our Minds, It'll Be,
Forever In Our Hearts,
This Fantasy…………..

These Memories

These Memories, I Have In My Head,
I Write Them Down,
Instead Of Re-Living Them,
Memories In My Head,
Good Ones, Bad Ones, Instead Of Getting Down,
It Helps Me In The End,
Of My Loves And Dreams,
It Always Seems,
The Dreams, Always Win,
Never To Go Back,
It's Fact!
These Memories, I Have In My Head,
I Write Them Down,
As I've Grown,
Memories Have Gone,
More About Loved Ones,
Nothing Bad,
Nothing Sad,
These Memories In My Head,
I Write Them Down,
My Secret Desires,
My Heart Fires,
As I Think Of Long Ago,
Where Did They All Go?
Oh! Memories,
Please Come Back To Me!
My Sweet Dreams…………These Memories…

Do You Think Of Me?

Do You Think Of Me?
I Often Wondered What It Might Have Been?
Too Often I Go Back,
For In The Past,
It Was Not Perfect, So Now I See,
Too Young At Start,
Afar And Now Apart,
This Is How It's Now,
Too Late To Try,
Many A Tear I Cried,
Over This Love, So Long Ago,
It's Too Late,
To Admit A Mistake,
I Think Of You,
Everyday It Seems,
Is It The Same For You?
Many A Year Has Gone By,
Water Under A Bridge It Seems,
Many Tales Not Told,
Do You Think Of Me?
What May Have Been?
A Love That Said Goodbye…

Once Had A Love

I Once Had A Love,
A Love, Now Lost,
It Meant Everything,
Now, Pain And Agony,
My Heart, Was On Fire,
This Love, Was My Desire,
My Heart Is Broken,
Words Have Not Been Spoken,
This Love, I Thought, Was Meant To Be,
Now My Heart Is In Pieces,
Memories Are Sad,
Remembering Nothing Bad,
I Keep Asking Why?
Through These Tears, I Cry,
This Agony And Defeat,
Oh! Makes Me Weak!
It Was Love, That I Seek,
A Love, So Unique,
Instead, A Broken Heart,
So, Far Apart,
Time Will Heal,
With This, I Must Deal,
I Wish You All The Best,
Love Will Find Us Again, Life's Big Test,
I Once Had A Love,
And Now This Love, Has Been Lost…

What May Have Been

*Often I Think,
Of What May Have Been,
A Love That Was So Deep,
Those Memories,
Of Perfect Harmony,
Holding Hands,
Walks In The Sand,
Love That Was Full Of Passion,
A Love, So Full Of New Sensations,
I Loved Her, She Loved Me,
True Love It Was Meant To Be,
Mistakes Were Made,
I'd Take Back That Day,
Push Rewind,
Put It All Behind,
Just To Have Her Again,
Imagining, No More Pain,
You Don't Realize What You Miss,
Until It's Gone,
A Love So Brief, So Full Of Kisses,
Now, Forever Gone,
Often I Think,
Of What Might Have Been,
Where Did This Love Go?
Where Did This Love Go?
For Reasons Unknown,
Love Has Died,
All I Do, Is Cry,
Knife To The Heart,
Twisting And Turning,
Love Has Gone Away,
Though, My Love For You Stays,
Love Starts Hot, Then Turns Cool,
I Pity This Fool,*

Love My Desire,
It Burns This Fire,
Words Of Hate,
Turn To Fate,
Words Of Rejection,
Give You Satisfaction,
Memories All I Have, So It Seems,
What Love Still Means,
Love, I Thought Was To Be Forever,
Instead, Ended Soon After,
It's All A Memory To Me,
All A Broken Dream…

Denied Love

A Love You Deny,
Love Has Died,
Baby I Tried, It Hurts,
My Broken Heart,
 You Say Wait And See,
I'm Afraid It Can't Be,
Tears I Cry,
I Wish I Could Die!
Every Day, I See You,
Why Is Love Untrue?
I Can't Play This Game,
Love Is So Far Away,
I See It In Your Eyes,
Can You Deny It?
Mixed Emotions A Many,
What Drove This Love Away?
I Wish To Make It End,
Loves Mixing Up My Head,
No Time For Me,
So It Seems,
Love Can't Be This Way,
I Will Think Of You, Everyday,
You'll Have The Biggest Part Of This Heart,
Baby, I Can't Take Anymore Hurt................

Chapter Two- Love

Little Words

Little Words I Write,
Of Love's Sweet Delight,
Secret Passions And Desires,
Hearts On Fire,
Of Love, We Never Tire,
Sweet Kisses,
Happiness And Bliss,
Dinners And Candlelight,
Starry Nights And Moonlight,
Long Talks And Long Walks,
Of Dreams And Fantasies,
Life's Tenderness,
And Life's Sadness,
Heartache And Loneliness,
Little Words, I Do Write…

Test Of Time

Our Love, A Test Of Time,
Love So Divine,
Everyday I Love You, Even More!
Words Of Love, Everyday I Swore,
First Time We Met, I Fell In Love With Those Eyes,
A Feeling Came Over Me, I Wanted To Cry,
You Walked Away, I Noticed The Rest,
I Thought, Surely She's The Best!
We Parted Ways,
Soon To Meet Another Day,
A Date Was Arranged, Much To My Delight!
Words Were Spoken, Though I Was So Shy,
Dinner And A Movie Date,
Holding Hands And Kissing, It Was Great!
My Heart Was Beating,
My Hands Were Shaking,
For My Love Was True,
My Love Was For You,
Two Weeks Went By,
Marriage Was Asked, Yes Said You, We Cried,
A Family We Began,
Off To A Town Faraway, We Ran,
Many Years Have Gone By,
It's Still You And I,
Every Time, I Look At You,
I Say, I Love You!

Whispers Of Love

Whispers Of Love, I Say To You,
I'm So In Love With You, You Know It's True,
Beating Hearts Together,
Love Forever,
Holding Hands,
Together, We Get Sad,
Love Songs That Are Ours,
From Each Other, Never Far,
Love You! Said Everyday,
Times Said, Are Many!
Smiles When We Talk,
Smiles When We Walk,
Always Hand In Hand,
As We Cross This Land,
Everyday My Love For You,
Grows So Much Stronger, Oh So True!
These Whispers Of Love Go On…

Loves Last Song

Loves Last Song,
About A Love, So Strong,
Love Starts So Easily,
Time Together, Oh Joyfully!
Every Word, Is Heard Carefully,
Love Spoken, Oh So Tenderly,
Little Things We Do,
Whispers Of, I Love You!
Long Walks,
Long Talks,
Love Is In Our Hearts,
Is This How Love Starts?
Long Summer Days,
Voyages Away,
Long Cold Winter Nights,
Cuddling Together In Bed, Oh Sweet Delight!
Getting Down On My Knee,
Asking, Marry Me!
The Answer Is Yes!
Oh Sweet Bliss!
Plans Are Made,
About A Future Date,
We Stroll Down The Aisle, Hand In Hand,
A Life Forever, Loves In My Head,
What The Future Holds Is Unknown,
Let This Song Be Told…………

Faded Memory

Loves Faded Memory,
Loves In The Back Of My Head, All History,
First Loves, So Kind,
Love Never To Die,
Little Things, Played Like A Scene,
Oh! What It Meant To Me,
Time Has Passed,
Faded Love In The Past,
Loves Faded Memory,
Loves In The Back Of My Head, All History,
Life Goes On,
The Thought Of Love Passed, Makes Me Strong,
It's All A Faded Memory To Me,
Little Things Remind Me Of A Love, That Was Meant To Be,
What Was Done,
Can Not Be Undone,
Time Heals,
I Do Not Think Of Love, Oh! So Now Bitterly!
Love Comes To Me,
Oh! So Easily!
I Have Met, This Girl Of Mine,
With Her, I Will Spend The Rest Of My Life,
For Love Has Found Me,
Loves Faded Memory,
Loves In The Back Of My Head, All History….

What Do I Say?

What Do I Say?
What Do I Do?
When I'm Alone With You.
The Things You Say,
The Things You Do,
Each And Everyday,
I Can't Wait,
Until I'm Alone With You,
Miles Apart,
But, You're In My Heart,
So Close, So Near,
But, What Do I Say?
What Do I Do?
When I'm Alone With You,
Many Words Spoken,
Many Questions,
When We're Apart,
Just Give It A Start,
The Dreams, I Thought,
What Would Be Spoken?
What Do I Say?
What Do I Do?
When I'm Alone With You….
This I Think,
Each And Everyday…

Love Game

What Game Is Love?
This Game We Play,
Is It Love?
So Many Unknowns,
So Many Chances,
So Many Dances,
For That, We Maybe Sure,
An Infatuation At First,
A Love That Bursts,
Two Lovers At Beginning,
Like Two Actors On The Big Screen,
No Script, No Lines,
Though It Seems,
A Lot It Means,
Who Knows What Love Plays?
True Love Is Hard To Find,
But, That's The Best Kind,
Excitement At The Start,
Complacent Near The End,
What Is This Game Called Love?
It's Wild Embrace,
For You And I, So Full Of Grace,
So Many Unknowns,
So Many Chances,
So Many Dances,
You And I, This Reality,
May It Always Be True Love,
Until The Day I Die…

A Fantasy?

Is It All A Fantasy?
A Dream? Or My Destiny?
Was It All A Cruel Game?
With Names?
Or Is It Real?
That I Feel,
Tell Me What Is This…
Is It Love Or Pain?
This Reality Or Game,
Tell Me Its Destiny..
This I Feel…
Or Is It Unreal??
The Truth We Seek,
Truth Will Reveal,
Tell Me, Tell Me, What You Feel,
For Its Real, This Love For You And Me,
Tell Me, Its Not A Fantasy But, Reality…

You Are My Life

You Are My Life,
My Burning Light,
When We're Apart,
You Are In This Heart,
Dreams Unfold,
Words Are Told,
Anytime You Are Near,
I Want To Hold You, Oh So Dear!
A Vision Of Loveliness,
Oh Sweet Happiness!
Love Has Come To Us,
Love That Trusts,
A Love, That Will Stay,
Destiny, I Say,
Love That Never Grows Old,
Hearts That Never Go Cold,
Every Minute, I Think Of You!
I'm So In Love With You!
Hold Me In Your Arms,
I Give You My Heart,
You Are My Life,
My Burning Light,
Never To Be Apart............

What Love Does To Me

What This Love Does To Me,
It Brings Me To My Knees,
Many A Tear,
A Love So Dear,
Emotions Out Of Control,
Hearts A Racing, Not Slow At all,
Hands A Shaking,
Body A Trembling,
Oh, What This Love Does To Me,
Can You Feel?
Feelings Of Love Dance In My Head,
To Never End,
When We're Apart,
Oh, My Beating Heart!
I Can't Help, Feeling This Way,
Every Minute, Everyday,
Together, Forever,
Love Forever, Together For Eternity!
Without You, There Would Be Emptiness,
A Void In This Heart, Such Loneliness,
What This Love Does To Me………….

Candlelight

Candlelight Dinners At Night,
Every Night For You And I,
Holding Hands,
Shadows Dancing,
Flames Flickering,
Hearts Are Beating,
Words Of Love Spoken,
The Past Forgotten,
Looking Deep Into Eyes,
There Are No Lies,
Passions Begin To Stir,
Loves So Much In The Air!
How Much We Mean To Each,
Talk About Life Together, What It Means,
Music Playing, Oh So Sweet!
Tender Kisses,
Sweet Caresses,
Love, So Softly,
So Tenderly,
This Love Meant To Be,
Together You And I, For Eternity,
Candlelight, Oh So Bright!
Show Us The Way And Guide Us Into The Night…

Little Things

Little Things We Do,
Little Things, Oh So True,
Stolen Glances,
Slow Dances,
Nice Hot Kisses,
This Business,
Little Thing, Called Love,
It Came From Above,
When I Met You, Our Eyes Met,
Gazed Oh, So Deep! That Was It,
I Fell So Hard,
My Desire, Oh My Heart!
We Met That September,
I Knew Then, It Was To Be Forever,
Emotions Ran Wild,
Though It Took Awhile,
Love Came,
Forever It Will Remain,
Our Only Desire,
Baby, Our Heart's Afire!
We Start Our Life's Adventure,
Which Path We Go, We Do Not Know For Sure,
Following Our Hearts We Go,
To What End, We Do Not Know,
Two Of Us Together,
It Will End, Never,
Little Things We Do………

Where Have You Been All My Life?

Where Have You Been All My Life?
Before You, Oh! So Much Strife!
You Have Always Been In My Dreams,
So It Seems,
Was It Fate? I Believe Its Destiny!
That Brought You To Me,
It's Like I've Known Of This Day Forever,
That Brought Us Together,
Life Before, Was Just A Rehearsal,
Ahead We Venture, No Reversal,
Angel Of My Dreams,
I Lived To See,
Sweet Destiny,
In My Dreams,
All Of My Life It Was Meant To Be,
This Love For You,
Oh, Sometimes Makes Me Act Like A Fool!
It's Love In My Heart!
I Feel Like We Are Never Apart,
Even We Are, A Connection Is Made,
For This Love, So Blows Me Away!
Where Have You Been All My Life?
Right Here Before You, Open Your Eyes…………

Rainfall

Rain Begins To Fall,
Sweet Rain At Night,
Clouds Move Away,
The Rain Moves, So Slowly, Away,
The Moon, So Bright,
Casts It's Light,
Over This Dark Night,
It's Glow, Illuminating The Sky,
Moonlight Glowing On The Droplets,
They Shine Like Diamonds, So Tenderly,
The Fresh Smell Of Rain, Washing All Sadness And Troubles Away,
Oh, It Takes Me To Another Day!
Sadness And Troubles All A Past Memory,
Moon Begins To Disappear,
Dawn Soon Appears,
Morning Fog All Around,
A New Day Has Been Found,
All The Troubles And Sadness Never To Appear..

Morning Sun

The Sun Shines In The Morning, Oh, So Beaming,
I Lay Awake As It Cuts Through The Trees,
For Everyday,
A New Day,
As I Think Of Love, A Smile Comes Across My Face,
It Seems, Just Like Yesterday,
That I Met You, It Still Seems Like A Dream,
To Speak These Words,
Words Of Love, Which Have Been Heard,
The Sun Shines In The Morning,
Thoughts Of Love, Oh, So Warming!
Of A Life Together, Oh, Sweet Desire!
You Are My Life, My Everything,
Without You,
I Would Not Know What To Do,
A Fire Within My Heart,
Oh, So Burning!
Life With You, Would Be So Carefree,
Together For All Eternity!
The Sun Shines In The Morning,
With You, Who Needs The Sun?
You Are The Sunshine Of This Heart,
Forever And Ever,
Together, For Eternity………

This Love

Of This Love We Have,
It's In My Heart,
Always Fresh, Always Free,
Look Into My Eyes, You Will See,
My Love Runs So Deep,
For Life Is Too Short,
Never To Be Apart,
For This I Feel,
Always In My Heart,
It'll Always Be,
Look Into Your Heart, You Will See,
My Love For You, It'll Be,
Of This Love We Have,
Search Your Soul, You Will See,
Of This I Am Sure, Yes It Will Be,
Always Fresh, Always Free,
Look Into My Eyes, You Will See,
My Love Runs So Deep,
Open Your Eyes, You Will See…

One Night

A Night Of Passion,
Friends They Began,
Words Spoken To Each,
Over Time An Attraction,
Who Makes The First Step?
That Is Not Said,
They Talk About The Moon,
The Stars And Soon,
Two Hearts Together,
And Thereafter,
They Soon Embrace,
That's All It Will Take,
That Fine Soft Hair,
Those Kissable Lips, I Swear,
Soon It Was A Great Scene,
It Was Hard To Believe,
The Soft Light Shown,
As They Proceeded Into The Unknown,
Soon To Be Familiar,
They Pour Out Their Desire,
Bodies Gleaming With Sweat,
Will It Ever End?
As His Lips Explore,
Every Place He Adores,
In The Soft Candle Light,
It Lights Up the Alabaster Skin Of The Goddess,
She Is Like A Beacon,
One Night
Glowing In The Candle Light,
There Is No Reason,
To Stop With This Delight,
Back And Forth, They Go,
There Is No Need To Keep Score,
The Love They Desire,

It Was Grand!
Surely You Can Understand,
The Outpouring,
Of Raw Emotions,
As They Lay Together,
It Seems Like Eternity,
Feels Like it was Meant To Be,
As They Gaze Outside,
There Was Bright Moonlight,
A Deep Sigh Explodes,
They Realize, It Is Time To Go,
When Do We Meet Again?
Surely That Is Not The End!
For If He Had His Way,
He Would Sweep His Goddess Away,
Words Are Spoken This Night,
Who Knows How It Ends?
One Night Of Passion,
Please Let It Be!
The Start Of You And Me!
Lovers At The End,
One Night
Filled With Desire,
Hopes And Dreams,
It Shall Be Seen,
Lovers We Will Be,
Together For All Eternity,
Promises Made,
Futures At Stake,
There Is Nothing I Would Do,
Just For This One Night To Last Forever With You…

Obsession

My Obsession,
My Dream,
Oh What It Means!
Is It A Drug?
Or Is It Desire?
This Longing, Between You And Me,
I Can't Explain It, Just Maybe,
It's The Ultimate Desire,
It's Controlling Me,
I'm Shaking Like A Tree,
You've Brought Out The Fire,
My Only Desire,
Call It Obsession,
Call It A Dream,
Oh What It Means!
There Is No Denying It,
You Feel It Too,
This Burning Desire…

Off The Shore

Off The Shore,
Far, Far Away,
As He Gazes,
As He Thinks Of More,
Seeking The Unseekable,
His Heart Wants More,
His Words They Speak,
His Body Is Shaking,
His Mind Made Up,
Of What He Desires,
This Burning Heart Aflame,
As He Gazes Offshore,
The Wind Carries His Thoughts,
To That Land Afar,
Reaching Out,
He Shouts,
Was It Fate?
Or Was It Destiny?
That Brought You To Me?
As He Reaches For The Sea,
Off The Shore,
Far, Far Away.........

Love Meant To Be

A Love That's Meant To Be,
Once I Saw You, It Was You And Me,
You Spoke,
That's All It Took,
One Look Into Your Eyes,
As I Cried,
I Knew It Was You And I,
A Love That Is Meant To Be,
A Love Deep From Within,
Forever And Ever,
It Was Meant,
It Will Never End,
For This Love Meant To Be,
As The Years Go By,
This Love Will Never Die,
Just Between Us, You And I,
For It Was Destiny,
That Brought Us Together,
And It'll Never End,
The Love That's Meant To Be…

Love Meant To Be

A Love That's Meant To Be,
Once I Saw You, It Was You And Me,
You Spoke,
That's All It Took,
One Look Into Your Eyes,
As I Cried,
I Knew It Was You And I,
A Love That Is Meant To Be,
A Love Deep From Within,
Forever And Ever,
It Was Meant,
It Will Never End,
For This Love Meant To Be,
As The Years Go By,
This Love Will Never Die,
Just Between Us, You And I,
For It Was Destiny,
That Brought Us Together,
And It'll Never End,
The Love That's Meant To Be…

Mystical Love

A Love That Is Mystical,
Love That Is Not Typical,
You Want As Much As I Do,
For That's True,
This Love That's Unique,
The Best We Can Do,
A Love That's So Deep,
Oh! The Chills, I Get!
When I Think!
The Mention Of Your Name,
I Go Almost Insane!
The Quivers,
The Shivers,
Am I Sick?
Yes! I Think!
For Eternity, I Wish!
For In Your Arms, I Dream,
This Love Mystical,
I Hope You See,
What This Love Means…

A Great Life

A Great Life,
With You, By My Side,
As Our Dreams Unfold,
Nothing Untold,
For It Is True,
This Love For You,
Many A Night Of Desire,
Oh, How My Hearts Afire!
Every Time Before I Fall Asleep,
My Last Thoughts Are Of You, Oh, So Deep!
Like A River,
Oh, So Goes My Desire!
Having You Laying Next To Me,
Please, Let It Not Be A Dream!
Until My Last Breath,
Until The Very End,
You Are My One Desire…

A Love That Will Be

A Love That Will Be,
A Love That Will Be Free,
Your Love For Me,
I Return To Thee,
No Questions,
No Guarantees,
Of This Love,
I Have For You,
For This Is True,
This Love That Will Be,
That Brought You To Me,
This Love That Will Be…

A Walk

A Walk, We Go,
Where Do We Go?
Let Destiny Choose,
We Follow The Clues,
A Bright Sunny Day,
A Lot To Say,
A Walk, We Go,
The Wind Blows, So Freely,
Words Come So Easily,
So Easy, When I'm With You,
Always It Is True,
As We Walk The Inland Sea,
Your Hair Blows Free,
Our Hearts, Full Of Glee,
My Longing For You,
Is….So True,
The Sand, Burning At Our Feet,
The Heat, The Heat,
Of This Midday Sun,
Just This Love, It's So Fun,
May It Be Always?
This Walk, Going Far, Far Away!
For This Heart,
Wishes, We Were Not Apart,
A Walk, We Go,
Where Do We Go?
For Eternity,
This I Know,
A Walk
Sweet Serenity,
I Know It'll Be,
My Only Wish,
Is A Kiss,
Kiss For All Eternity,
I Long For Reality,
Just For This Walk..

Darkness....

When The Darkness Falls,
I Can See All,
A Certain Planetary Star,
I Sit and Stare,
Is It Venus?
The Sweet Breeze Blows,
So Softly, So Softly,
Like a Gentle Kiss,
For That Is The Way, Love Goes,
I Think I'd Be Amiss,
If She Feels The Kiss,
It's So Dark On This Starry Night,
Oh! Venus, Look Into My Eyes And You Will See...
The Love Between You And Me!!
When The Darkness Falls,
Love Can Conquer All,
For If Loving You, Is A Sin,
I'm Guilty, I Profess!
For The Wind Always Blows...
Caressing My Soul...

Dreams

Dreams, Which Inspire,
Dreams Of My Desire,
Dreams, Which Bring Me,
Closer To My Heart, I See,
For It Is True,
These Dreams, About You,
So Real, So Alive,
These Dreams Of My Desire,
Dreams That Inspire…
These Dreams That Have Me On Fire…

Emotions...

Emotions Or Lust?
As Words Are Spoken,
Words Of Trust,
Straight From The Heart,
Unhindered, Unbridled,
Words Of Lust,
Raw Emotions,
Separated By Miles Far Apart,
Words Of Trust,
These Emotions,
A Grand Notion,
For It To Be,
We'll Have To See,
Answer Me This Part,
Is It From The Heart?
Cause Words From The Heart,
Have A Way Of Coming True,
Emotions, I Speak For You,
Have Come From This Heart,
Raw Sweet Emotions,
I Spoke For You…

Good Morning...............

The Day Starts With A Smile,
As I Lay In Bed, Awhile,
The Sun, Oh So Bright!
It Warms With It's Light,
My Thoughts Are Of A Girl,
My Heads, A Whirling,
Just The Thought Of Her,
Do I Dare?
Express My Desire?
As I Rise,
I Watch The Sun Rise,
I Pour Some Coffee,
Thinking. Oh, So Deeply!
As I Look Outside, Take In The Scenery,
I See, Pretty Greenery,
I Think Awhile,
Of My Love Through The Miles,
It Brings Good Memories,
Which, Will Ever Be....
A Good Morning, Indeed!

Hold Me

*Hold Me Until The Night Comes,
Hold Me In Your Arms,
We'll Forget About Life,
Dreams Are All We'll Visualize,
Hold Me All Night,
It'll Be Right,
But, Hold Me,
For You See,
Dreams Will Be Reality,
Hold Me, Make It True,
Hold Me, There Is Nothing,
Nothing, I'd Do,
To Make Our Dreams Come True,
Just To Hold You,
Hold Me,
Hold Me, Next To Your Heart,
Because When I'm With You,
Everything Seems Right,
Hold Me,
Just Hold Me All Night....*

Hope

Hope, I Dream,
Hope, I See,
Two Strangers Learning To Love Again,
In My Dreams, I Ran,
Far Away, Yes I Can!
Faithfully,
Truthfully,
I Speak Of This Dream,
Though It Seems,
Hope Will Become Reality,
I Long With Anticipation,
Oh! How My Soul Aches!
Waiting For That Day,
Which Will Not Be Too Far Away,
For This Is My Hope,
Hope, I Dream!
Hope, I Dream!

May It Be

May It Be Always,
My Love For You,
I Can't Help Feeling This Way,
Forever And Ever, That's True,
Two Different Worlds,
With These Words,
I Say,
I Can't Go Another Day,
May It Be Always,
My Love For You,
I Can't Help Feeling This Way,
Ever And Ever For You,
My Feelings, I Can Not Hide,
I Can't Keep Them Inside,
Without You,
Every Thing's Blue,
May It Be Always.............

Moonstruck...............

The Moon Light So Bright,
As He Looks Far Away,
Oh So Bright, Was The Light!
Off In the Distance, He Sees A Wondrous Sight,
Twas a Lady, Dressed in White,
Her Hair, Oh So Fair,
She Was the Lady Of The Moon Light,
A Lovely Vision, I Fear Or Was It Trust?
Her Skin So Fair, He Forever Stared,
So Was He Moonstruck? Did He Dare?
Oh, So It Was,
A Lengthy Pause,
The Immense Warmth He Felt,
Deep From Inside, He Was Melting,
Deep With Desire,
For this Venus of the Sky!
He Would Gladly Give Up Earth,
To Soar Above and Fly,
Just To Spend Eternal Life!
With This Lady Of The Moon Light,
He Did Not Fear,
For It Felt Right,
Just To Spend One Night Eternal,
With The Goddess of the Moon Light!

Moonlight

As I Lay Here Awake, Here At Night,
The Moonlight Streaming In Bright,
I Gaze Outside Afar,
And Next To Me,
What Do I See?
A Fair Maiden, I See,
Draped In Moonlight,
Her Fair Skin, Bathed In Light,
The Moonlight, So Bright,
Her Hair,
So Fair,
The Moonlight Reflected In The Soft Glistening Of Her Skin,
The Light On Her Face,
Which Takes Me To A Place,
So Far Away,
To Another Day,
I Lay There Awake,
Dreaming About My Moonlight,
So Bright,
How Much She Means To Me,
And How Much I Love Her Thee,
If It Is A Dream,
Do not tell this to me,
Let This Be,
My Reality…
Together And Forever
Together And Forever,
Ever And Ever,
May It Be..
What It'll May?
For On This Day,
My Love For You,
Is Undefined,
That Is Forever True,

When I Think Of You,
Forever And Ever,
May It Be?
This Love For You, It'll Seem,
There Is No Denial,
I'd Walk Many A Mile,
Just To Hold You,
In The Moon Light,
It'll Just Seem Right,
This Love For You,
May It Be True?
Together And Forever,
Forever And Ever…
I'll Remain…

Hold You

To Hold You,
As I Think Of That,
You Know It's True,
Cause That's Where It's At,
A Dream Come True,
A Love That's Anew,
My Wish Is That, I Would Spend Eternity With You,
For My Undying Love For You Is True,
To Hold You,
What I Give For That,
When I'm Blue,
You Make Me Smile,
You Make Me Laugh,
Just The Thought Of A Love Like That,
I'd Walk Many A Mile,
Just To Hold You,
For Eternity,
In My Arms, You'd Be Safe,
A Wonderful Place,
This Dream Comes True,
As I Think About That,
Is It Fact?
I Can't Wait Until I'm Alone With You,
This Is True,
My Undying Love For You…
Special Words
Special Words That Are Spoken,
Never To Be Broken,
Between You And Me,
Right From The Start, You See,
These Words, So Free,
Words Of Desire,
Words That Set Our Hearts On Fire,
All Day, These Special Words, We Speak,

Just For You And I, You See,
For It's True,
These Words Of Love, I Speak For You,
Special Words That Are Spoken,
Never To Be Broken,
Deep Words From My Heart,
Spoken Elegantly, From The Start,
Words Of Desire,
Words That Set Our Hearts On Fire,
May It Come True,
Just For Us Two,
Never Far Apart,
Always In My Heart………

Road We Take

The Road We Take,
Life Is About Reality,
On These Roads We Take,
Wake Up, Life's Unreal!
Years Gone Bye,
I Don't Know, Is It A Lie?
Long Winding Road, It Is So…
The Twists And Turns,
Love Is About Yearning,
Friends You Make,
Make Mistakes,
The Road We Take,
Life's Reality,
Live And Then You Die,
Wake Up, Life's Unreal,
Walk It To The End,
Soon You Will See,
When It Becomes The End,
No Map To Guide, As You Will Be,
So Let The Journey Begin!
Right Up To The Very End!
For If This Life,
Full Of Love, Full Of Strive!
Only You Can See If It's Real Or A Reality,
The Road We Take….

Woke Up This Morning

I Woke Up This Morning,
Sun Streaming In, It Was A Wondrous Thing!
My Mind's Full Of Love,
Oh! So Much Love!
As I Lay There, Oh! So Dreaming!
I Feel, So Thinking,
Of The Love, I Feel For You,
Truly, Hoping, The Feeling Is Mutual,
Every Waking Moment,
Every Sleeping Moment,
Spent, Dreaming About You,
How It Feels, To Hold You, Oh! So True!
A Big Piece Of My Heart,
I Give To You, Never To Be Apart!
I Woke Up This Morning,
All I Could Think About, Was So Kissing You!

Melody

Melody In My Head,
It Plays About Life Ahead,
Chasing A Dream,
So It Seems,
Oh, Bittersweet Melody!
Melody Of Life Past,
Melody Of Life, Oh, So Fast!
How Does It Start? How Does It End?
This Rhyme In My Head?
It Starts, So Slowly,
Words Spoken, Oh! So Slow!
Little Things Done,
Little Words Sung,
This Melody In My Head,
Let It Be Said,
The Sweetest Melody,
Plays In Our Head!
Our Hearts, Beat As One,
Love Will Not Be Undone!
Chasing A Dream!
So It Seems!
Oh! Bittersweet Melody!

Thoughts Are Clear

My Thoughts Are Clear,
They Are As They Appear,
Words Played Over In My Head,
Silence Clears The Head,
Of Love Past, Love Present,
What To Do,
A Vision Or Two,
Complete Satisfaction,
Of What The Next Move May Be,
This Is Anticipation, So Surely!
So Clear,
Of What Is Oh! So Near!
But, So Far Away,
Of This, I Feel This Way!
Every Thought I Dream,
Is It, As It Seems?
My Stomachs In A Knot,
Why These Thoughts?
Is It A Dream? Or Is It A Fantasy?
It So Scares Me This Reality!
I've Never Been This Way,
That Make Me Feel Like This Day,
My Minds Racing, Way Out Of Control!
Until I'm Told,
I Really Don't Know,
Where Does My Love Go?

Let's Play

Oh, Babe Let's Play!
This Game We Say,
Secret Fantasy,
Sweet Ecstasy!
Together We'll Be,
Just You And Me,
How Will It Start?
This Affair Of Heart,
Sweet Desire,
Please Never Tire!
Our Bodies, Dancing In Time,
A Little Wine,
Music Playing To A Beat,
Our Eyes, Oh! So Meet!
Oh, Baby Let's Play!
This Game We Say,
Secret Fantasy,
Sweet Ecstasy!
Our Bodies, Moving To The Beat!
Our Desire Meets!
Kisses Mingle,
Arms Intertwine!
Heart's Afire!
Oh! Sweet Desire!
Bodies Hot,
Sweat Happens A Lot!
Promises Met,
Words Have Been Kept
Let's Play
All Has Been Found,
Nothing Lost, Dying Love Unfolds!
Oh Baby! Let's Play!
This Game We Say,
Secret Fantasy,

Sweet Ecstasy!
As It Comes To The End,
Little Said!
In Our Arms We Lay,
Boy! What A Day!
Every Wish Fulfilled,
Every Desire Filled!
In The Soft Candle Light,
Stories Told, All Night,
Wishes And Desires Explained,
Promises Made,
Soon It Was Time To End,
It Was Time To Go,
I Wish, It Would Not End!
A Kiss Goodbye, So This Story Goes,
Tears Fell, So I'm Told, But This Is Not The End!
For This Love Never Dies,
Oh! Baby! Let's Play!

Regrets

Regrets We Have,
None, We Take,
Was Not A Mistake,
Secrets, Aplenty,
Lies So Few,
A Love We Have,
Regrets, So Very Few,
The Chance We Take,
Make No Mistake,
Oh! What Does It Take?
My Love For You,
It Could Be True,
I Promise This,
Sealed With A Kiss,
You Are My Only Desire!
The Mention Of Your Name, My Heart's Afire!
Baby, Give Me A Chance,
I'll Hold Your Hands,
To Never Let You Down,
No Regrets, My Love!
I Give You This Pledge On My Knees!
No Regrets, We Shall Not Have!
It Was Love, Not Far Apart,
Let Me Give You My Heart…

Showed Up

If I Showed Up One Day, With Roses In Hand,
Oh! So Grand!
What Would You Do?
Be Taken Aback? Or What To Do?
Flowers For The Sweet!
I Think It's Neat!
Would Dreams Come True?
Take You Away,
Sweep You Off Your Feet, A Great Day!
If I Showed Up One Day,
Roses So Grand,
Desires Realized,
Passions Finalized,
It's True,
A Dream Come True!
I Hope You Understand, Dreams Will Be,
Forever, Desires Seem Intense, That's A Fact!
When I'm With You, The Passion Erupts! That's How I Act!
If I Showed Up One Day, Roses So Grand,
Would You Understand?

Remember That Day

I Remember That Day,
Like It Was Yesterday,
Promises Made,
Promises Kept,
All I Ever Wanted Was You,
You Know That's True!
Words Exchanged,
Plans Made,
A Rendezvous!
Promises Made,
Promises Kept,
An Understanding,
A Helpful Hand,
Always There,
Not So Far,
Every Waking Moment A Smile,
Commitment Took Awhile,
Promises Made,
Promises Kept,
Every Blush! Every Look,
That's All It Took!
You Had My Heart!
Right From The Start!
I Remember That Day………..

Rest Of My Life

The Rest Of My Life,
I Give You That,
Through Every Strive,
We'll Walk This Life,
I Wish It So!!!
Oh! I'm So Outa Control!
I 'll Wait On You,
I'd Gladdly, Do It All For You!
What I'd Give, To Spend The Rest Of My Life!
Just To Have You By My Side….
Oh, It Feels, So Feels, So Right,
So Many Years, Years That Have Gone By,
Since I Have Felt This Way…It's No Lie!
The Rest Of My Life,
I Give You That,
Oh, Please Make It True!!
What I'd Give For You!
Every Kiss, Every Smile,
Brings Me, Oh So Close!
It's Been Awhile,
But, It's A Desire, I Feel,
I'll Go Down On My Knees,
Give Anything, Anything At All,
Just To Have You,
This Loves, Just So True.,
I'd Give It Up, All For You!
The Rest Of Life…

The Westerly Wind

*Let It Blow! Westerly Wind,
Bring Me Easterly,
Oh! Take Me To That Girl I Know!
As Sure As The Sun Rises,
Oh! Carry Me! Oh! Carry Me!
So Far Away!
Place Me, So Place Me!
Safe In The Arms, Of The Girl I Know!
Wind Take Me This Day,
I Can't Stay This Way!
Let It Blow! Let It Blow! Westerly Wind,
Bring Me Easterly,
So Gently! So Tenderly!
Westerly Wind!*

Voice Below

The Voice Below,
The Voice She Spoke,
Far Below,
She Sounded, So Sweet,
My Mind, It Did Not Believe!
It Was A Dream,
The Voice Below,
The Voice She Spoke,
Voice So Soft,
It Touched The Heart!
So Hot, My Desire!
Oh! Can't You Feel The Fire!
So Burning My Heart!
That Voice Below,
The Voice She Spoke,
Oh! So Sweet!
The Kind You Like To Meet!

Easy To Love

So Easy To Love,
Little Words,
Little Flirts,
Words Of Passion Spoken!
So Honestly!
It Was So, Meant To Be!
So Easily!
A Love That's Meant To Be True,
I'm So In To You,
Little Steps, We Take,
So, Slow, I Can't Take,
Just The Thought Of Being Near You!
Makes Me Lose Control,
Hands Are Shaking,
Minds Quivering,
So Easy To Love,
How Much More? I Do Not Know,
This Love Unfolds!
So, So, Out Of Control!

Sweet Angel

Sweet Angel Of Mine,
I Dream Of Time,
As I Close My Eyes,
Waves Of Emotions Flood Over Me,
Oh! I So Cry!
All I See, Is That Sweet Angel Of Mine,
Of This, I Tell No Lies,
Sweet Angel Of Mine,
Minutes To Hours Spent, Looking Ahead,
Of Holding Hands, Kissing, Squeezing,
This Angel Of Mine, You See,
If This A Dream,
Though, Know It Seems,
Never Wake Me,
Until, I See,
That Sweet Angel Of Mine!

A Flirt

A Flirt, Stolen Glances,
Smiles That Take Chances,
Sweet Things Said,
Stolen Moments Ahead,
Passions Allure,
Time Is Pleasing,
Little Things They Do,
Times A Wasting, Too Soon,
Stolen Glances,
Smiles That Take Chances,
Sweet Dreams All Night,
Last Until Light,
Spoken Words They Speak,
Oh! What Do They Seek?

Happiness

True Happiness, It's Fate,
It Began With A Date,
A Couple Of Drinks Poured,
All The Stories,
Of Love And Woe!
A Movie, We Go,
Touching Hands,
Attraction Is Grand!
Arms Around,
Kisses Exchanged!
A Night Passes,
It Was Good Bye!
So, Thought I,
Soon Again, Dates Many More,
Oh! How I Adore!
Two Weeks Pass,
I Soon Ask,
Will You Be My Wife?
Will You Be My Partner In Life?
True Happiness Is Fate,
It Started With A Date!
So Evermore,
I'm Still With The One I Adore…

As You Lay In Bed

As You Lay In Bed Today,
I Gaze At You, So Sleeping Like A Baby.
Every Day, I Say,
I Love You Always,
To Always Hold You,
It's A Dream Come True,
Every Night, I Hold You Tight,
So Much To My Delight!
Always Loving You,
These Words I Say,
The Meaning Oh! So True!
I So Feel That Way,
I Will Always Love You!
Forever And Ever, For Love Be True,
Until My Dying Days,
Oh! So Feeling This Way,
I Will Always Love You!

Things I Say

The Things I Say,
The Things I Do,
When Love's In My Head,
Thoughts So Clear Ahead,
Emotions Run Wild,
Passion Unfolds,
Regrettable Words Spoke,
This I'm Told,
The Things I Say,
The Things I Do,
All I Want Is To Make Sweet Love To You!
I Gave It All To You,
God! It Was So True!
All I Wanted, Was Happiness,
Oh! Sweet Bliss!
I Can't Tell You, How Much You Mean To Me,
Sweet Words, It Was To Be,
Forever, You And I,
We Flew To The Sky!
The Things I Say,
The Things Do,
Do You Know, What You Mean To Me?

Spread Your Wings

Spread Your Wings,
You Will See,
The Love For You,
Flying Forever, It's True,
Higher And Higher It Goes,
A Little Flame, Then So Slow,
Smoldering, Burning, Embers,
Flames Erupt To The End,
Spread Your Wings,
You Will See,
The Love You Have For Me,
It's In Your Heart,
Near But, Apart,
A Little Dance,
Oh! Take A Chance!
Never Too Late,
Let Love Begin This Day,
Open Heart And You Will See,
What Love Means To Me…
Spread Your Wings,
You Will See……….

Light Of My Life

Light Of My Life,
A Joyful Light,
Burns Into The Night,
You Are The Sun
Oh, So The One,
Light Of My Life,
You Are The Meaning Of This Life,
Your Smile, Our Desires,
A Taste Oh! So Acquired!
It Just So Seems To Me, I've Known You All Of My Life,
From That First Moment On, Sunshine,
Oh, Sunshine!
Light Of My Life,
Without You, Darkness,
With Dark, A Broken Heart,
Oh, Such A Joyful Sight,
When That Light, Fills My Heart,
It Fills This Soul, With That Sunshine,
Together The Voyage Starts,
Never To Be Apart,
Light Of My Life………

Unconditional Love

An Unconditional Love,
A Love We Have,
Words That Speak,
Words That Heal,
The Undying Kind,
Love Is Always In Our Mind,
What Is In The Past,
Baby, That's Last,
The Future We See,
Oh, What You Mean To Me!
An Unconditional Love,
A Love, Oh! So Strong!
We Hang On Every Word,
Every Day, A New Start,
Oh! Never, Never To Be Apart!
This Unconditional Love…

Chances

Chances We Take,
Choices Made,
Love Forever True,
Love, Like When I Met You,
Deep In This Heart,
I Knew You Would Play A Special Part,
Once It Started, It Could Not End,
Love So Strong, Playing In Our Heads,
Little Things We Do,
Written Words To You,
Little Tears Of Happiness,
Little Tears of Sadness,
Whispers Of Love Into The Night,
Togetherness In The Daylight,
Dreams Of Desire,
Hearts So On Fire!
Life Together,
Happily Forever,
Little Smiles Together,
Lots Of Laughter,
Chances We Take,
Choices Made,
Love So True,
I'm So In Love With You!

Circle

One Big Circle,
Life Is A Circle,
Mistakes Made,
Chances We Take,
Though Different Faces,
Sometimes, Life Sucks!
We Can Run,
But, Not Hide,
Are We Doomed To Replay?
Different Paths We Can Take,
And Not Make The Same Mistake,
For We Have Learned From The Past,
One Big Circle,
Life Is A Circle,
Take A Path And See,
Life Is Not Boring It Seems,
No Mistake,
No Retake,
Run The Path That Takes,
You, Into My Arms,
Forever More,
We'll Run This Path Together,
To A Sweet Destiny,
Life Is A Circle,
Run It And Come With Me..................

What Love Means

This Is What Love Means,
True Love It Will Be,
Honestly Loving Each Other, No Matter What,
Looking Into Each Other Eyes And Seeing What You've Got,
Waking Up And Saying" I Love You,"
Several Times A Day, Oh, So True!
Tender Kisses,
Oh, The Sweetness!
Love's Emotions, Happy And Sad,
Standing Together,
Supporting Each Other,
Holding Hands In The Rain,
No Secrets, What They May Be,
Massages At Night,
Oh, It So Feels Right!
Stolen Glances,
Slow Dances,
Whispers In The Dark, Saying, "I Love You,"
Cuddles In Bed, Taking Away The Blues,
Touching Each Other, Oh! The Electricity!
It Sends Shivers Down The Spine, Oh! So Tingling!
Growing Old Together,
Loving Forever,
Never Being Far Apart,
The Pitter Patter Of Hearts,
This Is What Love Means………

Roller Coaster

Love Is A Roller Coaster,
Climbing The Hill,
What's The Thrill?
Start So Slow,
Where Do We Go?
Holding Of Hands,
Taking A Chance,
We Hit The Peak,
Sweep You Off Your Feet!
Down We Go!
Oh No!
Emotions Reign,
Love Is So Insane,
The Bottom We Hit,
Is This It?
Whizzing Up Into Space,
Don't Lose My Place!
A Kiss Or Two,
Whispers Of, I Love You!
Hearts On Fire,
Sweet Desire,
Little Loops, Twists And Turns,
Oh, The Hearts Yearn!
Soon To The End, Or Is It The Beginning?
Go For Another And See What We Are Missing!
Love Is A Roller Coaster…………..

Cabin In The Woods

A Cabin In The Woods,
Far Away, We Would Be,
Just You And Me!
And Some Puppies,
We'd All Be Free,
Don't Let It Be Mistook,
All The Luxuries Of Life,
Very Little Strife,
Deer Will Play,
Right Before Us, In The Valley,
Warm Summer Days,
Cool Summer Nights,
Life Will Be Okay!
You Shall See!
Fire Burns, When No Light,
Staying Warm, It Shall Be,
Together Under The Blankets, You Shall See!
As We Gaze Up Into The Sky,
Just You And I,
Stars And Northern Lights,
Staring Up Into The Night,
Watching Everything With Delight!
A Cabin In The Woods You Shall See,
Just You And Me!
Our Warm Desire,
Shall Ever Be!
Like A Bonfire, Our Heart's Are So On Fire

Waiting

Always Waiting,
Sitting Here, Waiting My Time,
For The Love Of Mine,
No Matter What,
It's Love That I Have For Her,
I Will Gladly Wait For That,
So Waiting, So True,
My Love For You,
As I Sit Here, Writing Away,
Oh! Why Do I Feel This Way?
Thoughts Dancing In My Head,
Dreams Of What Lays Ahead,
Always Waiting,
For The Sweet Love Of Mine,
I Will Gladly Wait Until That Time,
For This, I Can Take,
So, Waiting For You,
Love Forever True……….

Who Chased Who?

Who Chased Who?
We'll Never Know,
Do You?
Simple Attraction, Started Oh, So Slow!
Words Of Passion, Words Spoke,
Unbridled Desires,
Oh! My Heart's Afire!
Do You Know What You Mean To Me?
So Many Passions You See,
A Simple Embrace,
My Hearts In A Race,
I Hope Not For Second Place!
The Sound Of Your Voice,
Do I Have A Choice?
The Mention Of Your Name,
Do I Have To Explain?
Where Do We Go?
Who Chased Who?
We'll Never Know,
It'll Never Be Known,
Desires Many,
Passion Aplenty!
I'm Samson You're My Delilah!
You're My Juliet I'm Your Romeo!
Lovers In The Beginning,
Lovers At The Ending,
Who Chased Who?
Let It Unfold!

Look Into Those Eyes
I Look Into Those Eyes,
What Do I See?
The Love For Me,
Oh, Those Eyes,

Eyes Of Mine,
Times Past, I So Wished They Were,
So, So, Turned My Way,
The Day, The First They Turned My Way,
I Looked,
One Look, That's All It Took,
I Realized That I Was Hypnotized,
So Mesmerized!
By Those Eyes,
Oh! I So Cried!
I Look Into Those Eyes,
The Love For You,
So Pure And True,
The Love So Much, In Those Eyes…

Love Like A Flower

True Love Is Like A Flower,
Different Types, Different Colours,
Each Unique, A Rainbow Of Emotions
Both Start From A Seed,
Each With Different Needs,
Warm Words Are Given,
Harsh Words Forgiven,
A Little Tenderness,
Warmth From The Heart,
Right From The Start,
A Little Rain,
And Very Little Pain,
As Shall Flowers Grow,
Love Flourishes After All,
Little Wind, So Gently,
Lots Of Kindness Tenderly,
The Flower And Love Stand Tall,
It's All True Love, After All,
True Love Is Like A Flower,
This Love For You And I,
Will Never Die…………………

Chapter Three- More Love

True Love / Dream

True Love, I Dream,
Though It Seems,
It Sometimes Eludes,
This Love, I Feel For You,
So Intense,
The Suspense!
Dreams About You, All Day,
Always Love, To No Dismay,
Sleep Doesn't Come Easily,
Awake At Night,
Sometimes Until Light,
True Love, I Dream,
Always Chasing,
Sweet Kisses I Have In Mind,
Love I Have, Do You Think In Kind?
My Heart Burns Of Desire,
So Hot Is This Fire,
What Is Next?
Sometimes I'm Perplexed,
Give Me A Sign,
Give Me The Time,
I'd Give It All Up For Your Love,
Leave It All For You, My Love,
Inside Me, A Feeling Of Heaviness,
Of Sadness And Happiness,
Blissfulness And Togetherness,
True Love I Dream
When I'm Near You, I Can't Control The Feelings,
One Thing Certain, I So Love You,
Say You Love Me Too,
True Love I Dream
Love You Can't Understand,
It's Like A Rubber Band,
Up And Down, We Go,

Twisting Until Tight,
Spins You Out Of Sight,
Emotions, Oh Out Of Control!
Where It Lands, Nobody Knows,
Making You A Priority At First, Then An Option It Seems,
Passionate At The Start, Then Fades Away Like A Bad Dream,
Burning Away, Then Gets Tight,
Releases It's Embrace, Then It Goes Out Of Sight,
Though It Seems, It's Not Right,
Boy! What A Ride!
Little Lies,
Big Cries,
Why Do We Love?
So Many Unknowns,
If Anybody Knows, Please Tell Me,
A Wise Person, You Shall Be…

Glasses Of Wine

Glasses Of Wine,
Words That Rhyme,
Music At Night,
Dinner Delights,
Music Has The Beat,
Love So Complete,
Arms That Intertwine,
More Glasses Of Wine,
Candles Burning,
Loves So Yearning,
Dancing Under The Moon,
Kisses So Smooth,
Love That Will Be,
A Love That'll Never Die To Me,
Love's Affection,
Love's Passions,
Dancing All Night,
Dancing Until Light,
Love Until The End,
Love For Eternity I Will Spend,
Glasses Of Wine,
A Wondrous Time,
Until The Very End....

Solitude

Deep In My Solitude, I Hide Away,
With My Thoughts For Another Day,
Wishes I Dream,
Always Dreaming It Seems,
Quiet And Dark,
Words Soon Start,
Questions I Ask,
Answers I Seek, Of The Past,
Love And All Of its Mysteries,
Of Dreams Or Are They Reality?
Seeking True Love Forever,
Happiness And Togetherness,
Solitude, I Seek,
Dreams, I Dream,
Of Sweet Love Ahead,
Oh Love In My Head!
Time Will Take Me Further,
Love Will Guide Me, Oh So Far!
I Realize Now, Love Has Found Me,
Open Your Eyes And You Will See,
It Was Here All Along……….

When You Close Your Eyes

When You Close Your Eyes, What Do You See?
Is It The Future? With You And Me?
Every Minute, Every Second,
I Dream Of This Love,
Of What We Have,
The Future I See,
A Pure Love To Be,
For Love Is Two,
A Love For You,
A Love For Me,
Can You See?
Give And Take,
Make No Mistake,
My Love Is True,
All For You,
I See A Future With You And Me,
Do You See? What I See?

The Future

What Does The Future Hold?
Plenty I Hope, As This Love Unfolds,
Loves I've Had, Not Many,
My Love For You, Aplenty,
I've Never Had Love Hit Me, Like This,
Did It Hit You? As I Wish,
A Deep Love, I Feel,
We Look Ahead, So Gleefully,
Sharing Our Dreams,
True Love, It Seems,
Loving Looks, Loving Arms,
That's All It Took, So Much Charm,
Don't Fast Forward This Love,
Old And Grey Together, With My Love,
Life's Big Journey,
Together And Forever, No Hurries,
Until The Day I Die,
I Will Love You! No Lie,
What Does The Future Hold?
As This Love Unfolds…

Love Spell

Love's Spell,
Oh How I Fell,
So Easily,
So Freely,
This Spell, The Power,
Words Of Love,
Of Desire,
From Within, The Fire!
Of Hopes And Dreams,
Everything, I Thought It Would Be,
So Full Of Kindness,
Of Happiness,
Right From The Start,
Be Still, My Beating Heart!
It Means So Much To Me,
This Love, Can't You See?
Love's Spell,
Oh How I Fell,
Is This Love? A Dream?
Please Say, It's Reality....................

Darkness Fell

Darkness Fell, Am I Alone?
Thought It Seems,
Thoughts Of Love, Comfort Me,
As I Write Along,
Filling Pages Forever,
I Write Of Love Together,
I Give You My Dreams,
Give You Reality,
Let The World Go By,
Let The Sea Go Dry,
Wind Will Blow,
Rain Will Fall,
Everything Goes Slow, Oh So Slow!
Let Karma Take It's Place,
We'll Do What It Takes,
A Love Meant To Be,
Angel Of My Life, You Mean So Much To Me,
Darkness Fell, Am I Alone?
Open Your Heart, It Won't Be Long…

Give For You

What I'd Give For You,
I Would Sail The Ocean's Blue,
Just To See Your Face,
Love Is A Race,
What I'd Give For You,
I Would Die For You,
Just To Hold You In My Arms,
Walk A Thousand Miles,
Keep Harm Away,
Just To See You Smile,
See The Sunset Together,
Love Would Last Forever,
Just For You,
Hold My Breath Until I'm Blue,
Send Roses, Everyday,
What I'd Give To You, Everyway,
Keep The Heart Afire,
Keep The Fire Burning,
All For You,
What I'd Give For You,
You Know It's True…
Like The Wind
Like The Wind, This Love,
Softly Blowing, So Gentle,
Which Direction, We Do Not Know,
Intensity, Which Way Does It Go?
Warm Or Cold?
True Love Holds,
So Fanning This Heart,
The Flames Of Love Spark,
A Gentle Breeze,
Or Is It A Hurricane?
It's So, Not Easy,
Love And Pain,

Sometimes Wild, Sometimes Tame,
Whichever Way,
My Love Will Stay,
Like The Wind, This Love,
Wind Take Me, Take Me To My Love....

Worlds A Turning

My Worlds A Turning,
My Heads A Spinning,
Oh! The Things We Do!
I'm So In Love With You!
When I Think Of You, My Body Starts Shaking,
Oh! The Earths A Quaking!
Worlds Collide,
Bodies Intertwine,
Oh! The Love I Feel!
It's Almost Surreal!
Days With You, Go By,
Earth Turns Day And Night,
Life Goes On,
My Love For You, Oh! So Strong!
For You, Are The One,
Our Two Hearts Beating As One,
Come With Me,
You Will See,
Destiny, And Reality,
My Worlds A Turning,
My Love To You, Is Burning………

Snowbound

Snowbound I Dream,
Of Love On A Beach,
A Love, So Magical,
Love, So Special,
Warm Air And Hot Breezes,
No Cold Breezes And Frigid Seasons,
Travel The World,
Dreams Put To Word,
Sweet Arms Embrace Me,
Sweet Love To Be,
Angels In Snow And Sand,
Angels So Sweet, Do You Understand?
To Live This, Is My Dream,
Dreams Become Reality,
Love In The Morning,
Love In The Evening,
Love All Night,
Love Until Light,
Oh Love, What You Mean To Me,
A Love So Strong! Can't You See?
Snowbound I Dream, So Wishfully,
Thinking Of A Love, Meant To Be....

Heartbeats

*Heartbeats In The Night,
Well Into The Morning Light,
Two Hearts, As One,
A Love That Can Not Be Undone,
Desire Held For That Special One,
Laying In Each Others Arms,
A Fire Burning, Oh! So Warm!
Hearts Telling Of Life,
Very Little Strife,
Of Each Others Desires,
Passions On Fire,
Hopes And Dreams,
Forever Happiness, It Seems,
Getting Lost In Each Others Eyes,
Exchanging Smiles,
Telling Of A Love, So Strong,
A Love, Not So Wrong,
Cuddling The Night Through,
Oh! So Much Love, I Have For You!
Heartbeats In The Night,
Well Into The Morning Light…*

Emotions

My Emotions, I Wear On My Sleeve,
Oh Can't You See?
I'm A Romantic, That's The Way,
Love Is To Be, Here Everyday,
Desire I Speak,
True Love, I Do Seek,
Dreams Are To Be Lived,
Dreams All Around In My Head,
Fantasy Becomes My Reality,
Dreams Are My Destiny,
Call It My Curse,
Sometimes It Just Hurts,
I Give And Give It All To You,
This I Give You The Truth,
A One Way Love At Times,
My Heart, So Pines!
My Emotions, I Wear On My Sleeve,
Oh! Can't You See?

Heart Of Mine

This Heart Of Mine,
I'm Just A Romantic By Part,
Always Dreaming,
Always Hoping,
I Fear, For That Is I,
A Fantasy,
For Reality,
Is Way Too Hard,
No Mistakes Made,
The Words Come Easily,
In This Fantasy,
My Intentions Clear,
This Heart Of Mine,
I Speak From Within,
Can't You Hear My Words?
I Want You Near,
Much Nearer Then You Want,
Over This I Am Wrought,
These Words from the Bottom of my Heart,
It's The Romantic In Me,
Why Can't You See?
This Heart Of Mine,
Over Time You Will See,
How Much I Feel…

Wrong Love

A Love That Is Wrong,
This I Say In A Song,
For My Love Is True,
A Love That Cannot Be Undone,
Like The Moon And Sun,
What Can I Say Or Do?
To Undo This Love Which Is Wrong,
Come To Me,
And You Will See,
For My Love That is Strong,
And You'll Forever Be The One For Me,
When You Make Love To Me,
There Is No Love That Is Wrong,
We Can Be Strong,
For Our Love Is Not Wrong,
For My Love Is True,
As Sure As The Sky Is Blue,
My Love For You,
Will Not Be Undone,
For You Are The Only One,
Come To Me,
And You Will See,
Forever We'll Be…

Reach For The Stars

Reach For The Stars,
Baby I'll Give You My Heart,
Only You Make Me Feel This Way,
Each And Every Day,
A Love, So Neat,
The Kind, You Can't Beat,
A Burning Desire,
A Kind Of Fire,
A Love For You,
Love Going Insane, Oh! So True!
When We're Apart,
We're Not Far,
Reach For The Stars,
Baby I'll Give You My Heart,
See The Signs,
Love That's Not Denied,
My Hearts On Fire,
Words Stroke My Desire,
Do You Hear That Beat?
It's My Heart, When We Meet!
Reach For The Stars,
Baby! You Have My Heart!!!!!!

Life's Lessons

Life's Little Lessons,
A Winding Road Of Sensation,
Love, Like, Hate, All Emotions,
Heart's Broken,
Love Stolen,
No Regrets, Just Lessons Learned,
Love Was Not My Turn,
Funny From Like, Goes To Love And Then Hate,
It's So More Then A Body Can Take,
Past Love Was No Mistake,
Past Mistakes Made, Without Them, I Would Not Have Found You!
No Regrets, Lessons Learned, How True,
From the First Time We Talked,
You Were On My Mind, So Walking Through,
Life's Little Lessons,
A Winding Road Of Sensation,
Until We Met, A Darkness Was Over Me,
Lightness Came, I Knew It Was Meant To Be,
A Love, So Strong, To Last Forever,
Words Came Out, Of Togetherness,
Baby, I Have No Regrets, Just Lessons Learned,
Life's Little Lessons, We Learn………….

True Love Found

True Love Has Found Me,
A Journey, It Has Been,
Once We Met,
That Was It,
No Others After More,
This I Swore,
Once You Have Found The Best,
Looking For Love, Takes A Rest,
Just Little Words It Took,
After Those, I Was Hooked,
True Love Has Found Me,
That's The Way It Is To Be,
No Broken Promises I Swear,
No More Broken Hearts,
Just My Undying Love For You,
Angel, That's The Truth!
I Give You All My Love, You Will See,
How Much This Love Means To Me,
No Sorrow, No Pain,
We Have Everything To Gain,
I Was Not Looking For Love, You See,
Once I Found You, That Was It For Me,
Words Of Passion, I Do Write,
Words For You, I Delight,
No Others Do I Love,
I Only Have Love For You,
True Love Has Found Me...

Give And Take

Loves Give And Take,
My Body Aches,
My Desire, Oh! How I Yearn!
Words Can Not Describe But, I Write The Words Of Desire,
I Wake Up In A Sweat, My Body On Fire,
Thoughts Of Love Anew,
Oh So True!
Everyday Thinking Of Loves Sweet Kiss,
It's Touched My Heart, The Tenderness,
A Kind Of Love, Never Felt,
No Regrets, No Guilt,
Loves Give And Take,
A Love We Can Make,
So Full Of Kindness,
Purity And Loveliness,
Only One Desire,
Our Hearts Are On Fire!
Words Are Spoken Everyday,
A Longing Desire Of Feeling This Way,
Love To Never End,
Loves Give And Take, Angel It Will Never End….

Dream Angel

Angel Of My Dreams,
She Comes To Me In My Sleep,
I'm Awake In My Head,
My Angel Beckons Me Ahead,
I Reach Out For Her,
So Reaching For That Hair,
Those Eyes Ablaze,
Sweet Music Always,
Angel Of My Dreams,
Where Have You Been?
With My Heart, She So Lightly Touches!
Love Surges, Oh So Much!
My Head Fills With Emotion,
I Think Of Grand Notions,
A Life Together, You And I,
I Do Not Want This Moment To Die!
Angel, Give Me Eternity!
You Will See, Our Destiny!
Angel Of My Dreams,
Oh, Come With Me,
Come With Me…..Angel…

The Ring

With This Ring,
It Means Something,
We Live Two As One,
Until The Day I Die,
It Will Be You And I,
Past Mistakes Have Been Made,
Life Has Been Kind Till This Day,
With This Ring,
I Thee Wed,
Until The Very End,
The Love For You, Is Still Afire,
My One And Only Desire,
Storms Come, Storms Go,
Which The Winds Blow,
Everyday We Say, I Love You,
Each And Everyday, It's So True,
Vows, To Which We Took,
Have Never Been Broken,
With This Ring,
It Means Something,
My Love For You, Will Never Die,
Words That Are Meant, It's No Lie,
It's You And I, To The End............

Every Morning

Every Morning, I Wake Up, Feeling Loves True Ways,
This With A Smile Everyday,
My Heart Full Of Desire,
Of This, I Never Tire,
This Is Love's True Ways,
It Takes Me Away,
Thoughts And Dreams,
About A Love, Oh So Deep!
May It Always Be,
This Love, For You And Me,
Every Morning, I Wake Up, Feeling Loves True Ways,
My Hearts On Fire, Taking Me Away,
Pleasant Thoughts, I Swear,
My Love For You, I Declare!
Love Has Bitten Me,
This Time For Eternity,
Loves Tenderness,
Oh Your Sweet Caress!
With A Kiss I Do Leave,
Thoughts Of How Much You Mean To Me,
I Will Love You Forever, It Is Meant To Be,
Every Morning, I Wake Up, Feeling Loves True Ways,
Oh Sweet Love Take Me Away!!!!

Love Poem

Love Poem, You And Me,
This Love For You, Oh So Sweet!
Every Minute, Everyday Thinking Of You,
A Love, So Pure And True,
Day And Night,
Darkness And Light,
All I Dream,
Is About You And Me,
You Are The Ultimate Prize,
That's No Surprise,
From That First Moment On,
A Love, Oh So Right, I Knew You Were The One,
A Love For You, With All My Might,
Much To Our Delight!
Love Poem About You And Me,
May This Love Forever Be,
Hearts Are Beating,
A Love With Feeling,
This Love, For You And Me…

Moonlight Awakens

The Moonlight Awakens Me,
Its Soft Glow Does Not Let Me Sleep,
It Reminds Of A Love So Dear,
The Kind Which, I Wish Was Near,
As My Mind Races,
Oh, Taking Me To A Special Place,
I Can Not Hope To Think,
Is She Thinking Too?
The Moonlight Bathes Me With Its Light,
Scenes Of Love Dance In My Head With Delight,
The Thought Of It, Seems So Real,
Dreaming Of What May Be,
So Awake Am I, Dreaming Of That Day,
Soon The Moon Falls Away,
The Moonlight Awakened Me,
Now Daylight Comes, Can We See?
How Much Love, I Have For You????

I Ask Myself

I Ask Myself, When Will You Be Mine?
The Answer, I Think Of All The Time,
A Love, Which Is Yet To Be,
Oh, What You Mean To Me!
Unattainable Love,
A Special Love,
Words We Speak,
Only Make Me Weak,
Actions Speak, So Louder Then Words,
I Do Not Want To Be Hurt,
Though Love Is Burning In This Heart,
I So Can't Bear Being Apart,
Thoughts Of You Racing In My Head,
It Makes Me So Weak Kneed,
The Thought of Denial, Makes Me Tremble,
Who Said, It Would Be Simple?
I Have Spoken Words Of Love,
No Return Of These Words, Which Have Been Sought,
It Doesn't Matter; I've Said It For Both Of Us,
I Hope You Feel The Trust,
And No Lies Have Been Done,
My Heart's On Fire For This Love,
I Ask Myself, When Will You Be Mine?
The Answer, I Think Of All Of The Time,
Very Soon I Pray!
I Cannot Wait For That Day….

What It Takes

I'll Do What It Takes,
To Make Dreams Become Reality, No Mistake,
All Of Our Hopes, All Of Our Dreams,
You Have No Idea, What You Mean To Me,
Life Together,
Reality Forever,
I'll Do What It Takes,
Climb The Highest Peak,
To Get What We Seek,
Swim The Rivers,
I Will Deliver,
A Hunger From Within, Fuels My Desire,
My Heart Beats, It's So On Fire!
I'd Walk A Thousand Miles,
Just To See Your Smile,
I'd Never Let You Go,
I Hope You Know,
I'd Take You Away,
Take You To A Special Place,
My Love For You, Is Not Denied,
Angel, That's No Lie,
I Will Do What It Takes,
To Make This Dream Become Reality No Mistake....

Guitar

My Baby, She Plays Me Like A Guitar,
Sometimes Softly, Sometimes Hard,
The Strings Of Love, So Tight,
Strumming My Heart, Into The Morning Light,
Totally In Tune,
All Night, By The Light Of The Moon,
It's Rhythm, Oh, So Unique!
Matches Perfect, To My Heartbeat!
My Baby, She Plays Me Like A Guitar,
Sometimes Softly, Sometimes Hard,
A Gentle Touch,
Oh, So Much!
Like A Symphony,
Its Quite Unique!
Guitar And Song,
Are Like One,
Each Keeping In Tune,
Playing That Song, About My Love For You,
The Way She Holds Me,
Oh, Can We Feel The Heat?
Emotions And Fingers Into Overdrive,
Playing, A Love, We Can Not Deny,
The Guitar Never Stops,
As My Love For You, Will Not,
My Baby, Plays Me Like A Guitar,
Sometimes Softly, Sometimes Hard,
Oh, Listen To The Beat!!!

Our Love

It Seems Like A Short Time Ago,
When Our Love Began To Glow,
It Seems Like Yesterday,
For It Was 25 years To This Day,
That You Said, I Do,
We Began Our Live Anew...
Through The Good And Bad,
All The Trials And Tests,
We've Come Up Surely The Best,
A Passionate Start,
That's The Best Part,
A Love, Which Still Remains,
To This Very Day,
Forever And Ever,
Always In My Heart,
As Strong As It Was In The Past,
And How It'll Forever Last,
For I Love You,
For You I Remained True....
This Love For You, Never To Die...

Free

Let Me, Be Free,
I'm A Free Spirit You See,
Of Love, I Dream,
For It Seems,
It Is My Dream,
A Hopeless Romantic From The start,
It's So In My Heart,
Of Love I Speak,
True Love I Seek,
Many Miles, I Travel For This,
Love Spoke, Oh! For What I Miss!
Of Love I Dream,
Gave Up Everything, So It Seems,
Just To Have You, In My Arms!
You Won Me, With Your Charms,
Let Me, Be Free!
I'm A Free Spirit, You See!
Only You Can Tame Me!

Many A Night

Many A Night,
I Lay Awake, Till Light,
Thoughts Of You,
So Alive These Dreams, So True!
A Warm Gentle Breeze,
It Blows So Tenderly,
Just Like Gentle Hands,
They Touch Me, Or So Warmly!
Many A Night,
I Lay Awake, Till Light,
Anticipate, So Eagerly!
My Thoughts Are Many,
Thinking, Oh! So Plenty!
Just To Spend My Life,
The Rest of It, With You,
Deepest Love, The Best, That Conquers All!
Oh! Please, Let My Life Be With You…
Many A Night,
I Lay Awake, Till Light,
So Dreaming…

Touch The Sky

Touch The Sky
You Will Fly,
Grab Your Dreams,
You Will See,
Travel Into The Great Unknown,
The Dream You Seek, Will Be Found,
Let The Wind Carry Your Dreams,
Love Will Be Found, So It Seems,
To Live The Dream Is Serenity Found,
Love Is, Reality,
Touch the Sky,
You Will Fly,
Grab Your Dreams,
You Will See,
How, Sweet Love Has Found Me!

Following The Dream

Following The Dream,
This Dream, I Follow,
Is Taking Over My Reality,
So Dreaming Of The Good Things In Life,
So Dreaming Of No Strife!
Happiness, I Have Found In You,
So Vivid, So True!
Travel The World, That Is The Dream!
Deep Satisfaction, It's To Be,
Conquering This Reality!
Is It Serendipity?
Please Say It Will Be, Dreams of Life!
A Lot To Ask, It Seems,
Do As I've Done, Look Into Your Heart,
We're Not Too Apart,
Following That Dream…………………

Winter Days

The Long Winter Days,
Are Fading,
A Memory, So It Seems,
Spring Is In The Air, So Gleefully!
Go From Cold To Hot, Snowing To Raining,
Deer Are Playing,
Birds Are Singing
What A Feeling!
Oh! So Joyfully!
No More Bitter Wind,
We Can See The End,
Nature's Love Around,
Passion, Oh! Surrounds!
Love, Oh, So In The Air!
The Early Morn, So Bright Of Stars!
A Cold Winter, A Distant Memory,
Warm Days Coming, So Surely,
The Future Comes Suddenly,
What Comes Next, We Will See,
Long Winter Days…………………

Morning Air

The Still Morning Air,
Words So Suddenly Appear,
The Beating Of My Heart,
Where I Start?
Speak Of Love,
Words That Fly, On The Wings Of A Dove,
Asking Myself, Why Can't I Have You?
True Love, For This Is True,
The Only Sound I Hear,
Is The Beating Of My Heart,
Oh, I Can't Stand Being Apart!
Thinking Of My Love For You,
The Future,
Of Us, Together, Never Apart,
Be Still This Heart!
The Still Morning Air,
Words So Suddenly Appear!

Things I Feel

The Things I Feel,
Of This Love So Real,
What I'd Give For You,
This Oh! So True!
I Dreamt Of Life,
Of You And I,
Together Happily,
So Blissfully,
The Things I Feel,
Of This Love So Real,
All Things To Be,
You Know, What You Mean To Me,
It Was Fate,
Not A Mistake,
That Love Was To Be Denied,
For You And I,
A Piece Of My Heart, You Will Be,
Oh! How I Wish You Could See!
These Things I Feel,
Of This Love, So Real,
Though Apart,
Many Tears Start,
Always In My Heart………

Jack Pot!!!!!!!!!!

To Dream,
It Seems,
Of Winning,
The Jack Pot, The Big Score!
This I So Wish For,
Close Your Eyes, Wish For More,
Open Your Eyes, You Will See,
Your Destiny,
Your Reality,
You Have Won,
Your Place In The Sun,
The Jack Pot!
The Jack Pot Of Love!
Of This I Believe,
No Riches, I See,
This Jack Pot,
The Jack Pot Of Love,
Look Into Your Soul,
You Will Attain Your Goals,
Of This, I Am Sure,
This Jack Pot, This Reality,
You Have Been Searching For..........

The Letter

Words Written Down,
Little Words With Meaning,
The Letter With Words, You See,
Words Written Until Dawn,
Words Of Passion,
And Of Commitment,
Of Love And Destiny,
Oh! Can You See?
Life Together,
Until We Part For Eternity,
Words Of Sensitivity,
No Fantasy,
Just Reality,
Words Of Hope And Joy,
Of Meaning And Happiness,
And Togetherness,
This, I Promise,
Said The Letter,
All For You, My Love,
Running Forever,
Like The Wind And Sea,
Go With Me,
For All Eternity,
The Words Said, Oh, So Tenderly,
Thus Spoke The Letter……………………………

Thoughts Dance

Thoughts Dance,
All In My Head,
Of Love And Happiness,
Soon Put To Words, You See,
Of Love And What it Means To Me,
Words Soon To Song,
Words, Not So Long,
Thoughts Dance,
All In My Head,
Into The Studio, We Go,
Not So Long, Ago,
Oh! Sweet Words! Of You And I!
A Concerto, Of Our Words!
Symphony Of My Heart!
To Words I Cry!
At My Love For You And I!
Tears That Never Seem To Dry,
At The Love That Will Never Die!
Music Put To Words, Oh, So True!
That State My Love For You….
Thoughts Dance,
All In My Head,
So Shaking My Hands,
The Thought Of You,
And The Future Ahead…

I Close My Eyes

I Close My Eyes,
Oh! So Awake,
A Little Piece Of You,
A Little Piece Of Me,
So, What To Do!
Sleep Does Not Come Fast,
Oh! I Need Some Rest,
Moonlight Dreams,
Moonlight Beams,
Keep Me Awake,
This I Take,
My Heart, So Aches,
How Much More, Do I Take?
A Love So Deep,
A Love So Strong, So It Seems,
Where Did It Begin?
How Does It End?
Never And Forever, It's Meant To Be,
I Close My Eyes And Dream Of This Love Meant To Be,
But, Oh! So Awake!
I Lay And Contemplate,
Moonlight Dreams,
Moonlight Beams,
Keep Me, So Alive!
Oh! So Alive………………

Key To My Heart

Only One Girl Has The Key To My Heart,
It Is Only Known To Her,
She Can Turn It Off Or On, As She Pleases,
Love Can Be Hard To Understand, Love So Teases!
With Her Love Can Be A Game,
A Love So Tame,
Love Can Be Hot,
Love Can Be Cool,
Love Is What We've Got,
Sometimes Cruel,
Hearts On Fire,
Full Of Desire,
Only One Has The Key,
That's The Way It's Meant To Be,
Love Is Off Or On, As My Love Pleases,
Love Has Struck Me…

If You Were Mine

If You Were Mine,
I'd Love You For All Time,
Loving You Each And Every Day,
This, I Promise, Without Fail,
We Make Love,
A Kind That Stands Above,
Your Wish, Is My Command,
In Fact, My Demand,
A Little Wine,
You Would Have All My Time,
Suppers For You,
With Nothing To Do,
Massages Aplenty,
Oh, For Eternity!
Long Walks,
Long Talks,
A Shoulder To Cry On,
Such Great Companions!
Many A Laugh, Nary A Tear!
Walks With The Deer,
A Dog Or Two,
A Cabin You Know,
Travels On The Go,
If You Were Mine…………

Run To Me

Run To Me,
You Will See,
It's Not A Dream,
Run With Me,
To A Distant Land,
So Hand And Hand,
Do You Understand?
Run To Me,
You Will See,
It's Not A Dream,
Promises Made,
Promises Kept,
I Plead My Case,
Many A Tear Wept,
But, You See,
Dreams Can Become Reality!
Run To Me,
You Will See,
Promises Kept...............

When The Morning Comes

When The Morning Comes,
What Is Done,
In The Night,
Soon Comes To Light,
The Day Is Young,
Oh! The Love!
Oh! So Strong!
Our One Desire,
Baby, Our Hearts Are On Fire,
We've Left These Morale Bounds,
A Love That Has Been Lost,
Has Been Found,
Every Step To This Day,
Every Play,
When The Morning Comes,
What Is Done,
Can't Be Undone,
My Only Desire,
Oh! The Fire!
Oh! Tell Me, Tell Me,
You Want More!!!!!

Second Chance

Second Chance At Love,
My Angel Is Giving Me Another Chance At Love,
Past Mistakes,
I Will Not Make,
This Time, I Know What To Do,
It'll Work, Through And Through,
Second Chance At Love,
We Don't Know What's Lost, Until It's Gone,
Every Minute, Every Moment,
Dreamt Of A Life Together,
This Time, Forever,
Oh! I'm So Glad!
To Be Given A Second Chance,
A Second Chance At Love!
I Was Confused,
So Afraid Of What To Do,
This Time,
This Time, No Mistakes,
My Love For You,
It's Pure And True,
Second Chance At Love,
My Angel Is Giving Me Another Chance At Love!

Love Race

Thoughts Of Love Race Through My Head,
I Do Not Look Back, Instead I Look Ahead,
What The Future Holds,
I Really Don't Know,
Chances Are To Be Taken,
Never To Be Unwavering,
All Loves I Think Of, With A Smile,
I Stop And Think Awhile,
Of This Love Presently,
Of How Much It Means Totally,
Thoughts Of Love Race Through My Head,
I Do Not Look Back, Instead I Look Ahead,
The Road Is Hard,
In The End, That's The Best Part,
All We Have Gone Through,
Love Is Worth It,
It Is True,
In The End, You Have It,
Open Your Mind And You Will See,
Oh! Sweet Surrender,
A Sweet Love For You,
So Present And Here,
Thoughts Of Love Race Through My Head,
Never To End............

One Life

One Life To Live,
It's Take And Give,
Love, The Ultimate Goal,
To Find It, Makes Life Complete, You Know,
Some Find Several Kinds,
Some Find Love, Forever In The Mind,
One Life To Live,
It's Take And Give,
Our Love Is Special, Kind And Gentle,
Life Was Not Complete Until We Met, Honestly,
Our Dreams, So Much Reality!
My Love For You Is Unconditional,
This Heart, Completely For You,
A Love That Is So Special,
This I Pledge, Oh, So True!
One Life To Live,
It's Take And Give,
A Special Kind Of Love, I'd Give Up My Soul…

Pain Sleep

As I Sleep Through The Pain,
I Call Your Name,
Though It Seems,
Even Asleep, Oh, What A Dream!
In My Dreams, I'm Running Towards You,
I Come So Close But, Yet So Far, Oh! What Can I Do?
This Broken Heart,
That Is The Hard Part,
Oh, The Pain!
When I Can't Have You,
It Drives Me Insane!
The Agony, It's True,
Thoughts Of Plans,
As I Thought, I So Ran,
Dreams Of What Brought Us Together,
How Love Is To Be Forever,
As I Sleep Through The Pain,
I Call Out Your Name,
Thoughts Come To Me,
I Know What To Do, It Will Come To Be,
We Will Be Happy Forever More,
Of That, I Am So Sure,
This Love Will Not Become A Faded Memory,
It Is Our Destiny, Our History,
As I Sleep, I Dream,
Of That Day, I Dream Away………………..

Chapter Four– Death

Angels Dance

Angels Dance Around In My Head,
So Vividly, Am I Dead?
I Wake Up Instead,
Realizing It Was A Dream,
Oh, So Real It Seemed,
Life Is So Close To Death,
A Short Time On Earth, Until Your Last Breath,
Until You Leave This Mortal Soul,
Where Do I Go?
After This Life?
Is Death, The Final End?
To That Last Breath, Life Is One Big Fight,
Some Survive, Some Do Not Try,
Angels Dance Around In My Head,
So Vividly, Am I Dead?
Warm Light Fills My Room,
So Bright, I Will Follow It Soon,
Do Not Cry For Me,
When I Die, It's Part Of Life You See,
Another Start,
Another Part,
A Life's Journey Of The Soul,
Where It Goes, I Do Not Know,
Angels Dance Around, All By My Side,
Angels So Kind, Guiding Me To The Light,
Wherever It Goes, It's Not Far,
Remember Me In Your Hearts............

Star..................

A Bright Star Has Joined Eternity,
As I Make This Journey,
Though My Life Was Short,
Too Soon, I Left This Earth,
My Friends, My Family,
Remember Totally,
I Will Love You All, With My Soul,
Through Circumstances, Beyond My Control,
Unable To Go On But, My Soul Lives On,
Remember Me, As I Was, Not As I Am,
The Good Times, I Had Many,
Bad Times, Very Few,
To Remember Me..
Look Towards The Midnight Sky,
As You See The Stars, The Twinkling,
It's The Twinkle Of My Eyes,
For Eternity, I've Become,
Do Not Be Sad, For Life Goes On,
Remember Me,
You Will See,
The Star, I've Become…

The Poets End

Until These Fingers Stop Permanently
And Life, As I Know It Ends Suddenly,
When I Get Carried Away,
On The Last Journey,
I Will Write About Love And Misery,
Through These Written Words, It'll Be,
About My Love For You, Oh! Do You See!
Leaving Your Sweet Embrace,
Though The Thought, Frightens Me,
Will Always, Be With Me, My Heart Still Races,
I Will Live On, In Your Memories,
Never Gone,
Never Forgotten,
One Can Not Change Circumstance,
Life Is One Big Dance
Just Remember, Your Love Will Carry Me,
Do Not Cry For Me, I Will Live On In Memory!

Chapter Five- Broken Love

Sunset

The Sunset Comes,
Another Day Is Done,
Thoughts Of A Love Afar,
Wishing On The First Star,
Wishing, Let It Be,
Always, You And Me,
It Was Love At First Sight,
Such Joy And Delight!
Things Soon Changed,
Love Hid Away,
A Broken Heart,
Oh The Hurt!
Thoughts Of You, Though I Try,
Tears Began, I Cried,
Love Needs Space,
What Could I Say?
Except, Try To Understand,
It's Hard To, When You Are Sad,
Love Is To Take A Break,
Of This, I Do Not Make,
Words Are Exchanged,
Promises Are Made,
Love Is To Be Put, In The Dark Recesses Of Our Hearts,
Placed In Our Memories, Always To Be Left, In The Dark,
Time Will Go By,
It Still Hurts, That's No Lie,
Friends We Remain,
Talking, Everyday...
Heavens Afar
I Look To The Heavens Afar,
I See A Falling Star,
A Wish, I Do Make,
One Wish, That's All It Will Take,
Place Me In Your Loving Arms,

Take Me, To A Land Afar,
Falling Star, Let Me Love Again,
Let Love Play In My Head,
Put This Heart On Fire,
Let Me Feel Desire,
I Have An Emptiness,
I Wish To Feel Happiness,
Only, If For One More Time,
I Look Into The Night,
Try As I Might,
An Empty Void,
Is In My Soul,
Love Is What I Seek,
It Will Make Life Complete,
Falling Star, Make My Wish Come True,
Bring Me Back The Love, We Once Had,
Let It Begin Anew,
I Look To The Heavens Afar, Oh So Sadly....

Walk Along

As I Walk Along,
I Think About What Went Wrong,
On This Dark Night,
The Moon's Bright Light,
Thinking Of A Love Gone Wrong,
A Love, Oh! So Strong!
My Hearts In Pain,
It Soon Begins To Rain,
The Spring Shower, Clears My Mind,
Thoughts Turn To A Warm Kind,
They Fill My Heart,
Oh, Why Is It So Hard?
Rain Turns Into Tears,
I Soon Preserved,
As I Walk Along,
I Think What Went Wrong,
Of A Love Gone Wrong.........

Feel Like A Number

I Feel Like A Number,
Always, Waiting In Line,
Do I Have The Time?
How Many Before?
Of That, I'm Not Sure,
How Many Behind?
Oh! Love Can Be Unkind!
Have I Lost My Mind?
I Feel Like A Number,
Always, Waiting In Line,
You Are So Gentle And Kind,
I Gladly Give You All My Time,
But, Baby, Something's On Your Mind,
Others You See,
Or So It Seems,
I Don't Know, What To Do,
Baby, I'd Do Anything To Have You,
I Feel Like A Number,
Always, Waiting In Line,
Have I Lost My Mind?
Am I Second Fiddle?
In This Quartet?
This Love Remains True,
But, If I Can't Have You,
This Number's Out Of Line!

Cross Roads

Cross Roads Of Life,
Like A Train Running,
Life So Passing By,
Is It Destiny?
Tell Me Why?
I'm Such A Romantic Soul,
Being Such A Fool,
Happiness Is Hard It Seems,
It Was Not To Be,
I Fell Too Hard,
That's The Bad Part,
Cross Roads Of Life,
Like A Train Running,
Life So Passing By,
I Stare Into The Abyss,
My Heart, Full Of Emptiness,
I've Come To The Cross Road Of Life,
Oh, Tell Me, Which Way Do I Go?
Please Guide Me, Where Do I Go?
The Answers, So Unknown....

I Saw A Face

I Saw A Face,
It Was Not Out Of Place,
Like A Butterfly,
It Was Sweet,
The Golden Hair,
The Lips Were Neat,
I Touched Them,
They Were So Soft,
So Supple, So Sweet,
Those Eyes,
The Hazel Kind,
The Lose Your Soul In Type,
The Dimples, I See,
Gentle And Not Too Deep,
What A Man Would Give,
To Touch That Face,
Nothing, Which Is Out Of Place,
I Give You My Soul, That Is True,
To Be Near You,
To Touch Your Face,
Oh The Thought Of the Embrace,
One Day, It Will Be,
The Sweet Surrender Of That Embrace…

Give It All To You

I'd Give It All To You,
My Love It's True,
No Questions I Ask,
I Would Take The Task,
Just To Be Near,
Oh Tell Me, That's What You Want To Hear,
I'd Give It All To You,
My Love All For You,
I Write Of This Everyday,
Love Guides Me On What To Say,
I Just Hope You Will,
Say That's Your Thrill,
When I Write To You,
A Love So True,
I'd Give It All To You,
My Heart Forever,
Wishing We Were Together,
That Day Soon I See,
Then It'll Be,
A Love For You, Never To Be Lost,
This I Give For You,
I'd Give It All To You…

Love Hurt

Love Can Hurt,
Love Can Burn,
It Twists A Knife,
Cuts So Deep Into Life,
Leaves A Hole,
In Your Soul,
Cry, I Do,
Over Losing You,
I Ask Myself, Why?
Oh I Could So Die!
Hurt Is Plenty,
Tears Are Many!
Try As I May,
Thoughts Are Sad, This Day,
Where Did Our Love Go?
This, I Would Like To Know,
Instead Of Happiness,
Tears And Sadness,
Do Not Pity Me,
I Will Get By, You See,
Love Can Hurt,
Love Can Burn,
The Fire Inside, So Fading…

Love Of Mine

This Love Of Mine,
Keeps Me Guessing All The Time,
Sometimes Smiling,
Other Times, I'm Crying,
Emotions A Many,
My Heads Going Crazy,
My Heart's Cold, Then Hot,
What Type Of Love, Have I Got?
Confusion Reigns,
Tears Begin To Rain,
What Do I Say?
Keep Silent, Hope Love Comes My Way?
I Can't Live Without This Love,
Can't Live With This Love,
Anymore, I'll Go Insane!
How I Pray,
Love Me And Stay,
Do Not Lead Me Astray,
My Feelings For You, Stay The Same,
No Matter What, They'll Remain,
This Heartache, I Can't Take,
It Just So Blows Me Away,
This Love Of Mine,
Choose Before It's Out Of Time…

Never

I'll Never Be Over You,
That's The Truth,
The First Time Our Eyes Met,
Oh! How I Wept!
I Found Love It Seemed,
That's What It Meant To Me,
Even So,
It Began So Slow,
Careful Steps,
A Few Disappointments,
Many Tears,
A Love, So Feared,
Something Happened,
We Took A Stand,
But, Understand,
No Matter What, I'll Never Be Over You,
Through And Through,
My Love For You, Will Never Die,
Until The Last Tear Dries,
Memories Will Remain,
Until My Dieing Days,
Time Spent Together,
In My Heart, Ever After,
I'll Never Be Over You………….
Just Remember, I Love You!!!

Shattered

Today, Dreams Were Shattered,
A Love, All In Tatters,
My Heart, So Hurt,
Dark Thoughts, Oh So Burn!
It Was Not To Be,
This Love Between You And Me,
With Determination, I Will Soldier On,
Tears Will Be Cried, Over A Love Gone,
In Sadness, I Cry,
The Only Sound,
Is My Tears Hitting The Ground,
An Empty Heart, I Felt, That I Had Died!
Sweet Memories,
Broken Reality,
Sad Thoughts Of Emptiness,
Of No More Togetherness,
A Broken Heart Remaining,
So, Filled With Pain…

A Broken Heart

A Broken Heart,
Many Tears, It's So Hard,
Life Without You,
Oh, Life So Blue,
What Can I Say?
Many Emotions, These Days,
Many Tears, I Cry,
A Choice Made, I Just Don't Know Why,
I Think Of Words Of Kindness,
Words Of Happiness,
Moments Together,
Love That Is Forever,
A Broken Heart,
Many Tears, It's So Hard,
When You Feel This Way............

When We Met

*When We Met,
It Was Quite A Hit,
Before Love Began,
Before Love Had A Chance, You Ran,
Love Was In This Heart,
Love For You, Which Never Had A Start,
Words I Say,
Words, Which Cannot Sway,
Time Will Heal,
Which I Thought, Was The Real Deal,
I 'm A Fool, I Thought,
These Emotions Of Mine, Are Overwrought,
It Was Love For Me,
For You, It Was Not To Be,
Was It A Game?
My Feelings For You, Were They In Vain?
True Love Only Comes Rarely In A Lifetime,
True Love I Felt, This Time,
Heart Beats Are Apart,
No More Starts,
It Was A Love, Never To Be,
Loves Bitter Memory…*

I See Your Picture

Everyday, I See Your Picture,
I Blow A Kiss Your Way,
I Cannot Deny, It's My Nature,
So Reminding Me, What Could've Been,
Instead Of Painful Memories,
A Love, So Magical,
So Mystical,
Everyday, Love Still Abounds In My Head,
A Love That's Alive, Instead Of Dead,
It's True, Love I Feel For You,
I'll Never Get Over You, Oh So True!
Walking Alone, Thoughts Of Love Gone,
Reminds Me Of That Love Undone,
Every Night, I Stare At The Picture Of You,
Before I Go, I Gently Kiss The Picture Goodnight,
Tears Come Easy, As I Close My Eyes, So True!
Dreams Of What May Have Been Echo Until Light…

Night Time

Night Time Will Come,
The Day Is Done,
Night Sky All Dark,
Dreams Will Soon Start,
Of Reality And Fears,
Love Brings Me To Tears,
Happiness And Sadness,
Loneliness And Togetherness,
Fight In My Mind,
There Will Be A Time,
When Everything Becomes Clear,
True Love, Which Is Dear,
Heartache And Its Headaches,
I Dream The Night Away,
Night Becomes Day,
Love Is Still No Closer..........

Torn Apart

Two Lovers Torn Apart,
A Tale Of Broken Hearts,
Love Denied,
Many Tears Have Been Cried,
A Love Thrown Away,
It Ended This Day,
For It Was Not To Be,
Bitter Love, I Feel,
Why? Is The Mystery,
Love That Is History,
Tender Moments, All Gone,
Love Has Become Undone,
Broken Hearts, No More Fire,
Tears Of Broken Desire,
Remember, I Will Always Love You!
You Know That's True,
Pieces Of This Heart, Put In A Dark Place,
I'm Crying, Night And Day,
Every Night, I Look To The Sky,
Gazing Upon A Certain Star, I Ask Myself Why?
Two Lovers Torn Apart,
My Love For You, Will Forever Be In This Heart…

How Do I Love You?

How Do I Love You?
Love So Hot, Then So Cool,
You Keep Pushing Me Away,
Why Is Love, This Way?
You Say, You Want Space,
Love For You, Is Confusing Me Many A Day,
Little Words, We Speak,
Oh What Do You Seek?
My Love Is Not A Game,
Crazy Love We Have Here Drives Me Insane!
Can't Stand A Day Without You,
Can't Stand A Day, With You,
Is It I? You Desire?
Does Love's Fire Burn Us?
My Heart's In Pieces,
Mind's Like A Rough Sea,
This, I Can't Take!
Is Love A Mistake?
Tell Me, How Do I Love You?

Visions

Visions Of Loneliness And Emptiness Fill My Head,
Feelings Of Unhappiness, A Love Now Dead,
A River Of Tears, I Cry,
I Keep Asking Why?
Where Did The Love Go?
The Answer, Still Remains Unknown,
A Perfect Love, So I Thought,
Instead, I Am Overwrought,
Instead Of Laughter,
I Feel Sadness,
Love Of My Life Said I,
Why Then, Did It Die?
Was It A Love Of Convenience?
Is It What You Seek?
Was It A Game Gone Too Far?
Was It A Dream? Whispering In The Dark?
It Was For You, A Dream, A Fantasy,
For Me, It Was Reality,
A Broken Heart, Little Pieces,
Hurt, I Do Feel,
Someday, You Will Understand…

Past Love

Past Love Has Been Let Go,
Past Love In My Head,
Past Love, Is Now Dead,
Present Love Is All I Know,
My Broken Heart Now Alive,
Never Again, I Do Strive,
A Long Journey, I Began,
At The End, I Stand,
Past Mistakes, A Faded Memory,
Begin Anew, This Life's Journey,
What Brought Me Here,
All My Tears,
A River Far Removed,
Happiness Is The Mood,
Sadness And Pain,
Are Forgotten This Day,
My Past, All Memories…

Lies

Little Lies,
Lies That Hurt,
Words Turned,
You Say One Thing,
Mean Something Else,
Little Lies,
Don't You Realize,
What They Do?
These Lies,
I Can See It In Your Eyes,
When You Tell Me Lies,
Words That Burn,
Words That Hurt,
Baby, You Are The One I Desire!
No Matter What, You Say Or Do,
Baby, I So Love You!
Tell Me, Tell Me, No Lies!
Take The Hurt Out Of My Eyes…………..

Love's Last Days

Love's Last Days,
Words Of Hate,
Like A Knife To The Heart,
Words That Tear It Apart,
Love's Last Breaths,
Almost Like Death,
Call It A Mistake,
This, I Do Not Say,
My Love For You,
A Love So True,
You Throw It Away,
Never To Be Another Day,
You Hold The Key To This Heart,
Threw It Away, That Hurt,
Fond Memories Will Remain,
Until My Dying Days,
Call It A Mistake?
This, I Will Not Say…

A Fool Was I

A Fool Was I,
Thinking I Could Find Love Again,
Tears I Cry,
How Did This Love Begin?
Emotions I Feel,
This Love Was The Real Deal,
I Thought Or Was I The Fool?
Started Hot, Then Gone To Cool,
Love In My Heart,
Now So Torn Apart!
Thoughts Of You, Make My Heart Jump,
Try As I May, In My Throat There's A Lump,
Drowning In My Tears,
My Thoughts, Not So Clear,
A Fool Was I….

Love Goes On

My Love For You Goes On,
Even Though, You Are Gone,
Nothing I Can Say,
Nothing I Can Do,
Will Make You Stay,
I Will Always Love You,
Sweet Memories I Will Dream,
Love It Will Always Be,
Though Apart,
You Will Be In This Heart,
For You, I Wish The Best Of Life,
All Calm And No Strife,
Time Will Heal,
What We Had, Was A Real Love,
Sometimes Sweet, Sometimes Sour,
Chocolates And Flowers,
Talks And Poems,
Hugs And Kisses,
Overall, A Strong Love For You,
Goodbye, It Must Be,
Please Remember Me,
My Love For You,
Will Never Be Gone…

The Day After

A New Day Is Rising,
Life With No More Surprise's,
Love Has Left Me,
It Was Meant To Be,
My Poor Heart,
So Full Of Hurt,
Life Will Survive,
Tears I Will Cry,
Heartache And Pain,
I Wish They Would Go Away,
So Many Things Left Unsaid,
Love Is Gone Instead,
Eyes To The Future I Go,
Where It Takes Me, I Do Not Know,
Love For You, All Hidden Away,
Never Again, To See The Light Of Day,
Hard As It May Be, Life Will Go On…

Chapter Six- Whimsical

The Poet

I'm The Poet, You See,
I Put Words To Paper, So Easily,
All The Emotions, I Write,
Comes To me Day And Night,
I Compose Of Love, And Desire,
It Sets My Heart Afire!
The Words Come So Freely,
I Write Of Love And It's Ecstasy!
Of My Loves Gone Wrong,
To Place It All In A Song,
Is My Secret Fantasy,
Of This, I Hope Joyfully!
It May Be Right Or Wrong,
To Put These Words Done,
From The Bottom Of this Heart,
I Write These Words,
So Others May Hear,
Of My Experience,
Of Love, Right Or Wrong.
For I Am The Poet, You See,
I Put The Words To Paper, So Easily…

Little Baby

A Little Baby Born This Day,
It's A Boy,
Such A Big Joy!
How Much Love On This Day,
With A Twinkle in His Eyes,
It Was A Big Surprise,
To See Such A Happy Family,
And As The Years Go By,
Baby Will Grow, This Is Reality!
Little Steps at First!
Then Big Footsteps!
With All This Love And More,
Of That We Can Be Sure,
Your Special Joy,
Will Be A Big Boy!
Baby We Wish You The Best,
For Daddy And Mommy's Love Never Rests!
Your Sweet Little Boy,
Your Little Bundle Of Joy!

Facebook............

Facebook, A Place Of Opportunities,
A Site, To Intermingle,
Oh! The Spine Tingles,
Click On,
Some Come To Make Friends,
Others For Love,
Some, Out of Boredom,
Common Interests,
People Galore!
Come For Someone Special,
Create Secret Desires!
Oh! The Fire!
Others Come For Opinion,
Just Click Go!
Stickers / Slickers,
All Types, You Know!
Some Broken Hearts,
That's The Hard Part!
Good Friends Made,
People Play,
A Million Requests!
A Thousand Notifications,
Oh! What To Do!
I'm So Confused!
Where's The Delete?
Invite Twenty,
I Don't Think So!
A Thousand Posts,
Facebook
Now I'm Lost!
My Computer Freezes,
I Thought This Was Easy?
God, Grant Me Serenity!
Before I Lose My Sanity!

Click Here!
Click There!
Please Help Me,
Let Me Be Free!
It Only Took One Click For Facebook,
And Now I'm Hooked!

Chapter Seven- Serious

True Friends

A True Friend Will Give Time,
Will Be A Friend For Life,
They Will Go Out Of Their Way, To Say Hi!
No Head Games,
Loves You In Every Way,
Over Looks Your Faults,
Gives A Shoulder To Cry On,
Comforts You, When People Die,
Cares For You, Like Nothing At All,
Comforts You In Times Of Hurt,
Takes Care Of The Heart,
They Make You A Priority, Not An Option,
Listens And Makes No Opinions,
A True Friend Remembers Special Dates,
Takes You To Special Places,
Shares Secrets, Only You Know,
With You, Grows Old,
People Come, People Go,
A True Friend Is With You, Forever…

Honesty

Honesty, With This Relationships Survive,
Totally With No Lies,
That I Give You,
Can We Be True?
No Lies At Start,
Straight From The Heart,
What Was The Past, Shall Be,
The Past Was, Shall We?
For Honesty, A Relationship Strong,
It'll Be Forever Long,
The Past Remains Unanswered,
That, You Can Be Assured,
Anew, We Can Be True,
This Love, So In Bloom!
I Give You My Heart, All My Soul,
Will You Give Me, The Same?
For I Have Lost Control,
Oh, Feel The Pain!
Time Immoral, You Have My Heart,
I'm On My Knees, Please Let It Start!
Honesty, With This Relationships Start,
So Totally True…

Spring

Spring Is In The Air,
The Sweet Sun Is Here,
Deer At Play,
Sun Everyday,
Snow Begins To Retreat,
Rain Begins To Beat,
Temperatures Soar,
Thoughts Of Being With Someone You Adore,
Leaves, Soon Appear,
Could Summer Be Near?
Grass Brown, Now Green,
Spring Is Here, So It Seems,
Sweet Birds Sing,
Oh Joy! Spring!!!!!!

Winter

Snowflakes Begin To Fall,
A Wondrous Sight For All,
Autumn's Leaves Disappear,
This Is The Time Of The Year,
A White Landscape,
Perfect Yards Snow Makes,
Temperatures Drop,
Furnaces On Hot,
Everything Has Ice,
I Really Think Its Nice,
Bears Hibernate,
The Geese Migrate,
Crisp Winter Air,
You Have To Dry Your Hair,
Winter Sports Prevail,
Bonfires At The Lake,
Hotdogs And Beans,
Fishing On Ice, That's Neat!
Cuddling At Night,
Watching The Northern Lights,
Snowflakes Begin To Fall,
I Wouldn't Trade It, For Nothing At All….

The Past..

Out Of The East They Came,
Towards The West, This The Way,
A New Life They Hoped,
All Their Dreams,
All Their Visions,
Headed Our Way,
Many Were Broke,
Onward Though,
A New Life Filled With Hope,
Through The Land Of Fields Of Gold,
Many Prosper And Many Went Broke,
It Wasn't Easy,
Things Never Came Easily,
But Their Visions, They Persevered,
There Was No Fear,
Only Hope,
A New Life They Hoped,
As Many Came, Many Died,
The West Was Wild,
Soon It Was Tamed,
By Many A Man,
This Great Land,
That Is Revered,
So Great And Wide,
Many Spoke With A Foreign Tongue,
Many Cannot Understand,
But, Over Time, Many Survive,
A Melting Pot,
They Called,
The Past…
This Great Land,
Only We Would Understand,
Of This Land We Call Our Own,
This Great Land Of Ours,

For The Fields Are Gold,
Our Streets May Not Be,
From Sea To Sea,
This Great Land Of Thee,
Just Remember, Many Came,
It's All The Same,
Many Came,
Many Stayed,
Many Died,
Many Went Broke,
But, All The Same,
They All Loved This Country In Name,
A New Life They Hoped,
Of Today Are Still Spoke,
A Melting Pot Yesterday,
Still The Same Today,
And Forever It Will Be,
From Sea To Sea………

This World

This World Of Ours,
I Question, Why War?
So Many Bloody Deeds,
So It Seems,
I Believe In The Kindness Of Mankind,
But, Why Is Life So Unkind?
Is It A Dream?
Or Am I A Dreamer?
How Many Dead?
Before It Ends?
Words Talk Of Peace,
Stop The Violence Please,
Actions Do More Then Words,
Love Is Better Then Hurt,
One Circle Of Fear,
So Many Tears,
Doomed To Repeat, Over And Over...........

Dream Catcher

Dream Catcher, Catch My Bad Dreams,
A Lot I Have, It Seems,
Of Love Gone Wrong,
Tell Me, Tell Me, To Be Strong,
Wind Carry My Dreams Away,
An Offering I Make,
Mother Earth Carry All To The Sky,
Let The Dreams Die,
Let Life Begin Anew,
Oh Let It Be True,
Heal This Heart,
Make It Not Hurt,
Guide My Path True,
And I Will Follow You,
Dream Catcher, Catch My Bad Dreams,
Show Me And I Will See…

Treat A Woman Right

Treat A Woman Right,
Respect And Cherish, So Much Delight!
Love Her With All Your Heart,
Comfort Her In Times Of Hurt,
Many Times, Say I Love You!
Love Her So True,
Equal Partners You Will Be,
Make Dinners Unexpectedly,
Lend A Sympathetic Ear,
Dry All Her Tears,
Dance A Plenty,
Take Chances, A Many,
Love Notes Everyday,
Take Her Away,
Hold Hands,
Long Walks In The Sand,
Show Her You Care,
No Secrets, No Affairs,
A Shoulder To Cry On,
A Love Never Gone,
Treat A Woman Right,
And Love Will Never Die…